Special Agent Sophia

SPECIAL AGENT SOPHIA

Mimi Barbour

Sarna Publishing

This is a work of fiction.

Names, characters, places, and incidents

are either the product of the author's imagination

or are used fictitiously, and any resemblance

to actual persons living or dead, business establishments,

events, or locales, is entirely coincidental.

Special Agent Sophia

The Undercover FBI Series – Book 9

Cover Art by Steven Novak

Contents

Dedication

This book was written for my best girlfriend, Carmel Anne – woman who's been in my life since our baby boys were born near the same time nearly forty years ago. She's a wonderful, warm sweetheart who's had to deal with a lot of heartache and yet... her tough spirit shines through.

She came to Rhodes, Greece with me and my family last summer. Two widows finding that life still holds fun times for them to enjoy. It was a special month, and deserves this story as a way to remember those precious days.

Stay safe, my friend.

xo

Praise

there and Sophie visited her often she was the perfect person to send. Sam the children 's Uncle would be there if she needed him. At first Sam and his sister wondered what the FBI was thinking of. Sending this silver haired beauty. After checking up on her Sam was sure she was the one.

As always Ms Barbour has created a wonderful story with wonderful characters. As always she draws me into her story and doesn't release me until the story is done."

~ Reviewed by Janine

"Loved this story. FBI Agent Sophia is sent on an assignment to Greece, which happens to be where her Yaya who recently passed away was from. In addition to the assignment she was working on and visiting family Sophia gets tangled up in a lot more than she bargained for. This is one of those stories that is hard to put down. Looking forward to more Undercover FBI stories." *~ Reviewed by TOZ820*

Reviews for Undercover FBI – Book #8: Special Agent Murphy:

"I enjoyed this story! It's a good addition to the "Undercover FBI" series of stand-alone stories. Passion ignites between partners. I love the characters and the plot is intriguing. It's entertaining and a good mix of action, suspense, passion, and romance. I look forward to reading what this author comes up with next." ~ **Reviewed by Mary**

"This is a great series! Great characters in each book and a storyline you'll love reading. Special Agent Murphy is a great addition to the series. You'll love the characters, the storyline is enjoyable to read and very well written."~ **Reviewed by buzymomof2**

"This book was so good and I have really been loving this series! Murphy and Kayti made such an amazing team, in and out of the field, and I loved that they seemed like an opposites attract couple with some amazing chemistry! Murphy is loyal, hard-working, shows a crusty side, but has a huge heart! And I really loved his protective nature when it came to those he loved. Kayti has a huge heart, a softer touch with those in need, but loved how she was like Wonder Woman when it came to kicking butt and wanting to protect others! I loved the case that they were assigned to, full of drama, mystery, and danger! This was a great romantic suspense book and I look forward to more from Ms. Barbour!" ~**Reviewed by Jessica N**

Praise for M. Barbour:

"As a writer myself, I think that one of the true marks of an excellent author is solid, believable character development, and in my opinion, Mimi Barbour is the master of character development!" ~ Reviewed by author Flo Barnett

"Love Mimi Barbour, love her books. When you can read a book that within just a few words, you are brought right into the book. You feel, taste, see everything going on. Great storylines. Fantastic characters, fantastic plots, storylines like real life both honest folk and of crooks. Humor that will have you giggling then full-on belly laugh. You may even shed a tear or two." ~ Reviewed by Shirleen Miller

Also Author of...

***All Mimi's books can be found FREE on Kindle Unlimited!!*

~*~*~*~

The Vicarage Bench Series
— Spirit Travel at its Best! —
She's Me (Book 1)
He's Her (Book 2)
We're One (Book 3)
Vicarage Bench Anthology (Book 4 – Books 1-3)
Together Again (Book 5)
Together for Christmas (Book 6)
Together Always (Book 7)

***

Angels with Attitude Series
— Angels Playing Cupid! —
The Angels with Attitudes Anthology (Books 1-3)
My Cheeky Angel (Book 1)
His Devious Angel (Book 2)
Loveable Christmas Angel (Book 3)
A Wonderful Life (Book 4)
Mischievous Christmas Angel (Book 5)

***

Elvis Series

— Truly a Christmas favorite! —
Holiday Heartwarmers Trilogy
Please Keep Me (Book 1)
Snow Pup (Book 2)
Find Me a Home (Book 3)
Frosty the Snowman (Book 4)
Love of my Life (Book 5)
A Perfect Storm (Book 6)
***

Mob Tracker Series
— She's unstoppable! —
Sweet Retaliation (Book #1)
Sweet Justice (Book #2)
Sweet Resolution (Book #3
Sweet Endings – (Book #4)
Sweet Faith (Book #5)
Sweet Leni (Book #6)
***

Single Title Series
He's My Baby (Book #1)
Christmas Runaway (Book #2)
Because You Cared (Book #3)
Daddy's Mine (Book #4)
Her Hero (Book #5)
You Make Me Happy (Book #6 – July 2020)
***

The Best in Romance Series
Red Hot Divas (Book #1 Box Set)

Hot and Handsome (Book #2 Box Set

***

Other Titles

I'm No Angel

Hotshot Cowboy

Big Girls Don't Cry

Christmas Runaway

The Surrogate's Secret

Mimi's Mix (Box Set)

'Tis the Season (Box Set)

Hearts, Flowers & Romance (Box Set)

Love, Christmas (Multi-author Box Set)

Unforgettable Romances (Multi-author Box Set)

Sweet and Sassy (Multi-author Box Set)

Unforgettable Heroes (Multi-author Box Set)

Unforgettable Christmas (Multi-author Box Set)

A Christmas She'll Remember (Multi-author Box Set)

Snowflakes and Christmas Kisses (Multi-author Box Set)

Unforgettable Valentine (Multi-author Box Set)

A Valentine She'll Remember (Multi-author Box Set)

Unforgettable Suspense (Multi-author Box Set)

Unforgettable Danger (Multi-author Box Set)

Unforgettable Trouble (Multi-author Box Set)

Unforgettable Weddings (Multi-author Box Set)

A Wedding She'll Remember (Multi-author Box Set)

Sweet and Sassy Brides (Multi-author Box Set)

Love, Christmas 2 (Multi-author Box Set)

Sweet and Sassy Suspense (Multi-author Box Set)

Unforgettable Thrills (Multi-author Box Set)

Unforgettable Passion (Multi-author Box Set)

A Romance She'll Remember (Multi-author Box Set)

Sweet and Sassy Cinderella (Multi-author Box Set)

Unforgettable Power (Multi-author Box Set)

Daring Protectors (Multi-author Box Set)

Unforgettable Charmers (Multi-author Box Set)

Sweet and Sassy Baby Love (Multi-author Box Set)

Sweet and Sassy Heroes (Multi-author Box Set)

Unforgettable Intrigue (Multi-author Box Set)

Unforgettable Christmas Dreams (Multi-author Box Set)

Sweet and Sassy Holiday (Multi-author Box Set)

Christmas Shorts (Multi-author Box Set)

Unforgettable Temptations (Multi-author Box Set)

Doctors in Love #2 (Multi-author Box Set)

Sweet and Sassy Daddies (Multi-author Box Set)

Unforgettable Joy (Multi-author Box Set)

Cute But Crazy (Multi-author Box Set)
Tempting Protectors (Multi-author Box Set)
Unforgettable Surrender (Multi-author Box
Set)

***

All Mimi's books can be found on her Amazon
Author Page:
http://bit.ly/MimiBarbourAmazon
OR
Website: http://mimibarbour.com

Chapter One

Special Agent Sophia Dunne stalked past two girls in the outer office and glared at them, saying without words that she found Maisie filing her nails an irritation; and Heather, who was giggling like a teenager on a personal phone call, an affront to what they should be doing in the FBI office.

When Suzi, one of the desk agents, followed, she found the two with their heads together, talking smack about the one person she wouldn't allow anyone to put down.

"What's up with you guys? Haven't you got any work to do?"

"Shit, you're as bad as the ballbreaker." Maisie threw a folder back into her desk drawer and slammed it with some heat. "Jesus! Can't a person file a cracked nail without getting the nasty eyeball around here?"

"Who had the guts to give you a nasty look?"

"Who else but your BFF."

"And me, I wasn't on the phone longer than a few minutes, just organizing dinner plans with a new admirer on eHarmony. So, sue me! Sophia's got such a stick up her ass, I bet she hasn't had a man take her out in years."

Suzi didn't want to let them talk crap about her friend. Not today, not after what she just found out. It wasn't in her to listen to this garbage without feeling the rub. If they only knew Sophia for the person she was, they'd shut their yaps. But she knew when to keep her own council and would have walked out if they'd have stopped there.

The two, giggling like bad girls in a high school cluster, kept up the bullshit – mean and full of self-righteous justification – and it cracked her resolve.

"You guys are so full of shit you make fools of yourself every time you open your mouths. Sophia has more heart in her body than both of you doubled. Remember last week when Lisa in IT was staring at an eviction notice because she hadn't made the rent for two months. It goes without question when a mom worries about paying for her kid's asthma medication or paying rent, it's a no brainer. Then she found out some anonymous donor had paid her back payments and even covered this month's rent. Well, it sure as shit wasn't one of you hyenas who stepped up, was it?"

"Seriously? Sophia did that? How did she know Lisa needed help?"

"She overheard the landlord on the phone reaming Lisa out and threatening her with eviction."

"How did you find out?"

"I was there. A few minutes after the call, Sophia left. A little while later, I had to call her out for that shooting on Main Street, and I heard the man in the background saying it was a good thing Lisa had friends because he didn't really want to make her leave. But he had bills to pay too. I knew where she was then."

Heather slapped her hands on the desk as if frustrated, her expression full of self-recrimination. "That convinces me."

"She'd kill me if she ever found out I'd let the cat out, but it burns my butt listening to you two go on about her when I know she puts *her* goodness and *her* money where *your* mouth is. So stop with the bellyaching and help her when she asks. Otherwise, mind your own fucking business."

"Son of a bitch!" Maisie piped up, shaking her head. "She's the last person I suspected; figured it was the boss, Bruner." The heavyset bleached blonde leaned back in her chair. "Look, Suzi, we'd be happy to friend her but it's impossible to get past the shield she hides behind. And even harder after they sent her to that training program in Texas, what's it called again?"

"You mean the ALERRT – the Advanced Law Enforcement Rapid Response Training program?"

"Yeah, that's the one. It's like she struts around with a superior chip on her shoulder all the time. And her hair freaks me out. How can someone so young have pure silver hair? Bloody stuff is natural too. I don't get it."

"You're crazy, you know that? Her hair's gorgeous and... she's fucking shy. If you talked to her once in a while rather than ignore the woman, you'd see that. And if your career meant that you were called out to every incident involving a hopped-up crazy with a gun, maybe you'd have your head in the job too. It can't be easy knowing your skills are used to kill someone."

Maisie added, "Yeah, but just remember, they're the bad guys who need to be stopped before they kill civilians. It's understandable who has to die. Plus, I've heard she opts to wound them almost every time. Come on... she's doing a necessary job."

"Okay, but you try going out there and put yourself on the line. See if you don't get a serious side."

Heather added, "And don't forget, she's one of the best we have in this state. Last week, she shot that asshole, Sopher, when he tried to hide behind a kid for heaven's sake. Who does that?"

Suzi began breathing easier knowing she'd turned the tide of their condemnation. Now they viewed her friend the way she'd always known Sophia to be. After all, if her silver-haired friend hadn't been on the spot when Suzi's own mom had shot up with the fentanyl-laced heroin, they'd have lost her. It was Sophia's grasp on the situation that saved the older woman. It was the night she'd come for dinner after numerous invitations. Then she'd excused herself right after Suzi's mom had gone out to meet up with a friend. She'd been the one who'd trailed her to a dark alley where she bought her drugs. And, she'd been there after her mom shot up.

If she'd have walked away, the injection would have killed her. But she'd called an ambulance and then hung around, making sure her mother stayed upright and conscious. When the ambulance showed up, she was able to tell them exactly what happened so they could administer the Naloxone that saved her life. They'd brought her mother back from the brink and Suzi felt a debt she'd never be able to repay.

How Sophia knew her mom was using, and she herself had missed it, still irked her, made her question her own abilities as an investigator. Sure, because of her injured leg, she worked mainly from the office, but she'd still been trained in Quantico like the rest of the agents.

The car accident that had her pinned in the driver's side for an hour before they'd found her caused not only her problems, but it was what led to her mom's later downfall. The opioids they'd given Suzi for her pain had sat in the medicine cabinet unused. Knowing how addictive they were had pretty-much stopped her from taking them. She'd lived with the agony until it became unbearable. She'd broken her resolve twice and resorted to the pills cut in half, welcoming the relief, and then pissed at herself for giving in.

It was her mother's back pain that led the older woman to go searching for some respite when she'd stumbled on the medication and had begun using it unknown to Suzi. That's the moment the devil had stared her mom in the face, and she'd succumbed. Suzi often wondered if she'd known how addictive they were. Nervous to know the answer, Suzi never asked.

Thanks to Sophia, today she was comfortable in a rehab facility that had convinced her to stay on in the position of a live-in therapist. Being a psychologist before she'd retired, her counseling skills were desperately needed for the folks who lived the same sickness she'd just overcome. Once she'd totally kicked her own habit, she could speak with the voice of one having gone through hell herself. After her back operation, it had all worked out.

It was one of those nightmares that eventually turned out to be the best thing that could have happened. And a year later, both Suzi and her mom thanked God for her friend's quick thinking and kindness.

Chapter Two

"The hospital called about Sopher. He'll make it," Bruner said. "And the lowlife bastard will spend the rest of his sorry life in a cell where he belongs, thanks to you, Sophia. You did a good job. One inch to the right and he'd have been a dead man."

"Trust me, I was tempted. Especially looking into his eyes and seeing a cold-blooded killer staring back, no humanity, no empathy for the terrified kid he used as a human shield. Or for the hysterical mom begging him to let her son go."

If the truth were known, it had broken Sophia's heart hearing the poor woman's screams for mercy for her little boy. That, and knowing the crimes that led up to the perp being hunted down and cornered, gave her pause as to whether she should just put him out of his misery. Make him pay for all the laws he'd broken most of his adult life and for the people he'd hurt and killed. Those facts played with her conscience for seconds before she pulled the trigger and did exactly what she knew she could do... wound. Not kill.

Her skills were such that she had no doubt she could place the bullet strategically. A very tiny window of opportunity. A split second of choice. The difference between her looking in a mirror knowing she didn't cave, didn't give in to her baser instincts for payback for his victims... the fact that she did the right thing by not playing God.

Bruner added, "I'm telling you true, Sophia. You're the only one I'd trust in that situation. Most would have gone for the kill-shot and slept like a baby that night."

"Trust me, bunny. I was tempted." She grinned in her special way that curled her mouth up on the one side enchantingly, not a look she often shared, but one that tended to delight the receiver. "All the red-tape afterward stopped me."

"Bullshit. You can't play the hardass with me, toots. I know you too well. I saw you take your first step, though no one in the company knows our background. And it's no one's business that your old man and I were partners back in the day."

"Ha, if the people here found out how I called you Bunny for years before I knew how to pronounce your real name, they'd never let it go."

"Your dad always called me by my last name, still does. A habit he has with everyone, well except for you and your mom. Bastard has some quirky ways, but he was the best agent I ever knew. Had instincts that were bizarre and the staying power of a freakin' pit-bull when it came to getting the bad guy. You're just like him."

"Sure, and he gave me his white hair too, didn't he now. Every time I go to visit, he has to comment on how much I look like his mother."

Bruner laughed, knowing how much Pat liked to tease. "I wish he didn't have to retire so young. That shot he took ruined more than his leg; it took his career. Him being a widower doesn't help. I worry about him out there in the backlands of Canada, living alone and spending his days fishing for crissakes. A man with a brain like his wasting away on fish."

"St. John's is not the backlands, and you know it. Newfoundland was his home as a boy, and he loves it there. Leave him be. The rest of the kids are all settled nearby with lives of their own, and he's missed Mom for years. Now he seems to be happy with his choice of a pastime. And you know he isn't just fishing; he's working on his fifth book and has made his place in the mystery market. His work sells better than many others working as an author, and it makes life extremely comfortable."

"Yeah, I know. I see them all over the stores, even saw one in Costco last week. I'm proud of him. He's done well, and he's gifted. Still... I have to admit the best job he ever did was bringing his oldest girl up to be like him. That's why I'm passing over a special assignment to you. One that most of the agents would give their first-borns to be detailed on."

Sophia slouched back in her chair, her long legs out in front and her sleek black boots crossed at the ankle. "Sure. It's most likely some shit job you haven't the guts to spring on anyone else."

"Aww, come on Dunne, would I do that to you?"

"That and more. Quit with the butter, or I'll let slip your nickname in the lunchroom. What's this fantastic job?"

Turning serious, Assistant Special Agent in Command Bill Bruner leaned back in his chair and crossed his muscular arms over a belly he'd been trying to get rid of for years. His busy grey eyebrows lifted, and his grin faded into his mustache and beard. Not being a big man made no difference to the respect his people had for him. They feared him, loved him, and most took his orders knowing he always had their backs.

The serious look that came over the beloved face made her wish she could go over and hug his neck like she would have done as a child.

"I'm sending you to Greece, leaving in the next few days. And you'll never guess where?"

She sat forward, excitement clawing at her stomach. "The island of Rhodes, right?"

"How the hell did you figure it out?"

"By the glint of excitement in your devious eyes. You know it's the island where Mom came from."

"That I do. It's also where our California Governor's husband, a powerful Greek tycoon, absconded with her two children – five-year-old twins, a boy and a girl. She wants them back. Unharmed."

"Can't she go fetch them herself? Surely it's something they could work out together without bringing in the FBI?"

"She tried and was stopped at the airport and refused entry. They rudely sent her packing."

"He must have some clout. Poor woman."

"Yep. After she returned and hired a professional to look into the matter, he recently uncovered the fact that her children's father is involved in a human trafficking ring based in Amsterdam. If she tries again, she'd be in a lot of danger away from the protection her position offers in the states. You're her hope of retrieving her kids. The woman's devastated. And right now, if the truth were known, with the economy tanking the way it is, we need her here. And we need you there."

"Jesus, boss. You can stop making me feel like I'm indispensable. You chose me because I speak fluent Greek and spent most of my childhood summers in Rhodes with Mom and Grandma."

"True." Bill leaned forward, and the power of his position and personality made her pay attention. "Besides your smart decisions on the job, you have a good brain, a strong will and you're stubborn like your dad. I can rely on your discretion and you never fail when you set your mind on something."

"Uh huh..."

"Plus, you own property there which gives you a reason for your trip."

"See, I knew you'd have an ulterior motive for the smooth-talking BS. Even I can recognize, it's a no-brainer for me to be the chosen one."

"Hell, yeah. Look, Sophia you're a top agent and the best shooter I've ever seen. You've won this department a lot of trophies and good publicity. I know I've had to lend you out from time to time when other states called for your expertise, but this time, it's our own Governor who's in trouble. And I want one of my best agents on the job."

Sophia's heart ramped up and excitement took over. It had been over a year since she'd returned to her favorite place on earth. After her grandmother's death, she'd arranged for the small villa she'd inherited to be rented to a family friend who recently decided to move to Athens so she'd be closer to her daughter and grandchildren.

Since then her house has been empty, and she'd played with the idea of returning on her next holiday anyway. Without her beautiful Yaya there to greet her in her loving way, it would be sad, but she owed it to her mother and grandmother to take care of the place they all loved so much.

"Okay. When do I go?"

"First, you have an appointment with Governor Reagan so she can fill you in on the details. Then you can gather what you need. Let's say in three days if you can get everything ready by then."

"Hell, Bunny, you know me. I was born ready."

"Good. And you call me Bunny one more time, kiddo, and I'll phone your dad and tell him what you're up to."

"Nah! You won't."

"No, I won't, but not because you deserve my pity. But because he'd be on the next plane following."

Chapter Three

Sam Reagan felt the pain that oozed in waves from his only sister, Governor Maureen Reagan. It filled the room and couldn't be dismissed as a minor issue, not when her heart was breaking. The blonde-haired woman hurt bad. The horror of having her children snatched from her arms had eaten away at her control so much so that anyone with any empathy sensed her grief.

He'd noticed wrinkles that had suddenly appeared around her light-blue eyes and the way her mouth stretched into a smile rather than in the past when the smile lit up her whole face.

The anger he felt at the man who did this to his sister made his stomach cramp with painful knots that he couldn't ignore, not when this person mattered more than anyone else in his life. She was all he had left, and he'd do anything to keep her and her kids safe and happy.

Words broke from him that he regretted as soon as they aired. "I told you he was an asshole when you first introduced me to him before the wedding." Sam's frustration showed clearly in his tone.

"Sure, you did. Five minutes before the ceremony."

"I was on a job and barely got my ass back in time to give you away. Christ it still drives me crazy thinking I missed your whole relationship leading up to the big day. It didn't help that you kept it from me. And then rushed the wedding."

"You know why. I found out I was pregnant. He insisted his children would be born legally. Like most Greeks, Manos grew up a strong catholic. Look, you were on a dangerous assignment and worrying about me wouldn't have done any good. Besides, his persuasive powers were incredible."

"Maybe. But you were a District Attorney at the time. You saw through people, had the knack of winning case after case. That's what earned you the vote when the big day came. Young as you are, people trust you. And you work your heart out for them."

"Maybe that's my problem. I worked so hard; I forgot my family needed me too."

Sam used a stern tone, his manner abrupt, "Jesus, Maureen, you did nothing to deserve this behavior."

She covered her face, her hands trembling. "We

had a good marriage at the beginning, Sam. Manos treated me fine for the first few years, especially because of the babies. He adored them. But I obviously didn't know the real man. His acting skills were that good. Eventually, he showed his true nature."

"How so?"

"He became abusive and mean. I made excuses – he worked too hard, had to be away from the family so much that it made him crazy. All the same excuses he whined about after he took out his irritation on me."

Sam roared his fury, "He hit you? That dirty, cheating bastard hit you?"

"He was building up to it. In the end, he'd push me and overpower me with his body trying to scare me." She couldn't tell Sam of the rape the last night they spent together. Her brother, her protective bodyguard from the time she was a little girl, would change from a man incensed to a man possessed. He wouldn't stop until he had revenge, and all she wanted was her children. She'd let the good Lord worry about the retribution Manos deserved.

"Scum like him don't change, Maureen. They can hide their spots, but they never completely disappear."

"Yes. And now my babies suffer because he's an arrogant, manipulative beast."

"I wished you'd confided in me earlier. You know I'd never have ignored a plea of help. I would have left the job and come home."

"He did too. It scared him. The thought of you returning and finding out about our life. I believe it's why he left when he did. I never told him you were on your way, but I found out later, he'd been reading my text messages. Probably got into my emails too. Thank God, the official ones are in a different laptop, under a separate code that's impossible to open without both a password and my handprint."

"It wasn't government secrets he was after. I told you, he's involved up to his scrawny neck with a human trafficking gang headquartering in Amsterdam. They have a whole network throughout the poorer countries in Europe. The funds involved are mind-blowing."

Maureen's eyes grew cold. She grimaced and shook her head. "It's ridiculously hard for me to believe the man who's so crazy for his own kids, the religious person I know could possibly be involved in such a horrendous crime."

"Human trafficking takes on all shapes and sizes. Most people believe their victims are young girls sold into prostitution. But that's no longer the case. They sweet-talk all kinds of people into leaving their countries to come to the States, work for rich folks who will pay their expenses. Sure, there is the hooker angle, both for the males and females, but many come to a life of pure drudgery. They toil for years earning low wages. It's cheap labor. They're told they can pay back the accrued costs of their journey and then find out after a nightmare trip those costs are astronomical, and it would take them many more years than they expected to repay what's owed. They basically become slaves to the bastards who turn a blind eye to get bargain help."

"How can humans treat other humans so callously? What kind of a world looks the other way? It breaks my heart to think I lived with a man, loved him at the beginning, only to find out he's part of such a disgusting scheme."

"People like him learn to play roles, sis. You've seen it in your work."

"Sure. But it's only supposed to happen to other people – not me. That prick used me for five years."

"Yeah, well it happens. Accept that it's his bad, not yours. Remember the refrain that as officers of the law we learned from day one. It's about the money... always is. People like him never think of the victims, just the profits. We'd been tracking this particular group for some time, so when I stumbled upon his name, I gotta admit, it freaked me out. That's why I came home."

"Thank God you did. I tried to find you after I couldn't get to the children myself, but you were in deep undercover on some mission. It's why I turned to Bill Bruner, an old friend. He promised the FBI will send in one of their best agents who, from what I understand, owns a house in Rhodes and can come and go without there being any flags put up at the airport. Manos obviously has connections on the island who'd contacted him to let him know I was arriving last week. I told you he put a stop to me, his own wife, getting past security. I was devastated when they forced me to return home."

Sam's voice vibrated with sympathy. Wanting to concentrate on the good news, trying to give her some hope, he said, "FBI? Good idea. They'll have no reason to suspect him. Agents travel a lot to different countries. Neither will they stop me. I'll use an alias. My firm sets them up all the time for the men when we need to go undercover. I'll be there, in the background and watching everything the agent does."

Maureen ran into his open arms and hugged him intensely. "I knew you'd help. It's why I haven't totally lost my mind." Tears appeared, and she had trouble talking while they filled her throat and gushed from her swollen eyes. "You know those two kids mean the world to me. I can give up anything else, my home, my job, but I beg of you, Sam, don't make me live the rest of my life without them."

"Come on, sissy." He used a pet name that always made her smile. "You know I'll win. I always do. It's why I own the biggest security firm in Florida. I don't have to tell you how unique we are and why all the best companies want our expertise.

You know yourself how busy I've been. But never too busy to look after my family. I'll bring Jack and Casey back to you, I promise."

He hugged her close and marveled at how strong a woman she'd become from the little girl who used to follow him around. Being only two years older, he let her hang out some of the time. But he put his foot down when they were teenagers and he was embroiled in getting with as many girls who'd open their young arms to the handsome kid with the flirty ways. His big brown eyes and slick tongue were so convincing, most didn't resist and the ones who did, he usually ignored.

Once she'd wiped up from her latest breakdown, he settled her back in a chair and made her listen. "I'm not going to be out front on this one. I want to stay covert. Therefore, I won't meet your agent today. I'll hang out in the other room, watching the monitor. The less he knows about me, the less likely there'll be any trail to alert Manos."

"Manos thinks you're still in Tehran. Or at least that's what he believed last week."

"Then let's hope he still believes it. There's no trace of my return. If he's keeping watch over my footsteps, he won't find anything. In the meantime, I'll be a shadow for your agent."

When the maid let her know that Agent Dunne had arrived, Sam turned on the cameras he'd placed around the room and then hightailed it to the den to watch on the monitor.

"Hello. I'm Special Agent Sophia Dunne. I'm here to help you recover your children."

Maureen stood and greeted her guest with a handshake and her public face well in place. She handled the shock of being approached by a gorgeous, tall, long-legged beauty with glowing silver hair quite well.

Chapter Four

Sam – not so much. When he saw the gorgeous female with her hand extended and a smile in place approach his sister, he leaned in close to the monitor, and his reaction exploded.

Son of a bitch!

What the hell kind of an agent had they sent to cover this case? She looked more like a model – tall, her legs shapely and slim, her eye-catching thick, pure white hair fanned out around her shoulders in a fashionable way the women wore today.

At first, because of the sleek silver mane, middle age seemed a reasonable assumption. Then she turned slightly his way, and her profile exposed young skin and perfect features that made him reassess. This girl couldn't be older than late twenties, if that. She was a freakin' baby agent they'd sent to take on a huge and possibly dangerous assignment.

What the fuck?

He couldn't take his eyes off her as his appraisal continued. The black leather jacket worked with the slim black pants, and she'd matched the boots to the jacket which gave her an appearance of a chic female in a movie setting not a sensible agent whose job it would be to solve the mystery of his missing niece and nephew.

The various necklaces she wore caught the light and looked feminine, a style most women couldn't pull off. On her, they looked attractive. As did the way she held herself.

He didn't realize he'd stopped breathing until she turned fully toward the camera and he got the first real glimpse of her face. He flashed to his feet, his fists forming. Son of a bitch, the blasted woman could stop traffic.

They needed to keep a low profile, sneak under the radar to get information about Manos and his group of lowlifes. This girl was an attention magnet. He'd hoped he could work with the agent, join forces with their intel and back up each other.

After seeing Agent Dunne, it looked like he'd be working alone most of the time. He guessed he could pull a few of his own staff from the jobs they were on, but as it turned out, everyone was placed in hot spots around the world, doing double the work because one of his teams had been ambushed on a job in Jersey with three being outright killed and five still recovering from an explosion.

Understaffed and overworked, they'd carried on as best they could. He'd also left his own crew short in Tehran and it worried him. Not being one to brag, he knew his skills were such that to replace him, they'd have to send three people. And they didn't have them. Jesus! He'd have to get the headhunters busy on a new recruitment process for more employees.

In the meantime, he had no choice but to plan a trip to Rhodes. And he'd have to find a way to interact with the princess the FBI considered one of their best. *Fuckin' seriously?*

He pulled his phone out, ignored the eight messages, and called the one person who got away with more bullshit than any of his other employees. When it came to researching anything both legally and illegally online, John, his tech genius, could be relied on. He'd skirted the law all his life, pulling so many underhand moves that it was only a matter of time before the authorities caught up to him.

When that happened, Sam had been notified. He'd been on the lookout for a man with John's special skills and had shared that bit of information with his sister, then the district attorney.

Once Maureen informed him that a genius computer crook had surfaced and was awaiting trial, Sam had stepped forward with a job offer the crook couldn't afford to refuse. Sam paid a top lawyer a hell of a lot of money to keep his new employee out of the slammer and over the years, he'd never regretted this decision.

He'd won the appreciation and admiration of the skinny, curly-haired gifted robot who never slept, very seldom ate, unless chocolate showed up in the food in some way or another, and had a romance going with a computer he'd built called Baby.

He'd put the guy on the payroll, set him up in a suite at the Hilton where the lazy sot never had to lift a finger to look after his own needs. A call to the hotel lobby took care of everything from room-service to whatever food cravings or other urges that might attack.

John claimed the privileged role of the most satisfied employee on his payroll. Protection from interference, or interruptions was kept to a minimum and he never did anything he didn't want to. While he had the best equipment money could buy, he sat surrounded by dozens of computers and remained on duty answering incoming calls from all Sam's people situated in all parts of the globe.

Lately, though, things had gotten so stressful; Sam had recently okayed the hiring of a younger guy genius to give him a hand with the constant onslaught. Unfortunately, they had the same first name and so the older one now became known as John-john. They switched the second name with the first for the younger employee who they now called David-john. Confusing, yes. But it worked for them.

"Hey, John-john. You got a few minutes to do a search for me?"

"Always. What's up?"

"I need you to find out everything you can about an FBI agent called Sophia Dunne."

"On it, boss. Shouldn't take long. I'll get back to you."

"Just send me a report on what you come up with. And its top priority, so put Baby in the closet and concentrate."

First John chuckled and then he said, "She's sleeping in. No problem."

Sam's groan made his employee laugh before he hung up. The kid loved pulling Sam's chain whenever he could and Sam let him because... well, because it gave John-john a few moments of enjoyment, and with his life being so limited, he deserved some fun.

During this whole time, Sam hadn't taken his eyes off the couple on the screen. He'd listened to the agent's discourse and watched his sister's reaction. At first, he knew the shock of her gender had been a bit of a letdown, but Maureen was used to dealing with uncontrollable circumstances. Her recovery had been quick.

And being a woman who herself held a huge amount of responsibility; she never showed any deference to men over women. Not like he did.

Though he had female soldiers on his team, and he'd worked with some of the best, he'd automatically assumed the FBI would send a male who could take on a snake like Manos Savas.

After all, the handsome face and muscular physique attributed to one of the reasons his sister had been conned, why any woman might be enticed. So why take a chance he'd sweet-talk Agent Sophia Dunne when his niece and nephew's future depended on the outcome.

In this case, his animosity for the wavy-headed bastard's treatment of sissy far surpassed his criminal activities for putting him behind bars. Only one thing would keep him from treating the man to the beating he deserved. When all was said and done, his father status to Jack and Casey had to be considered.

Chapter Five

Sophia dressed carefully to meet the Governor. She had started with her regulation FBI dark gray suit and her hair swept up in a roll, ugly medium pumps on her feet, followed by a ten-second stare in the mirror before she changed. That wasn't her, never could be.

Because she worked a lot on sites where life and death hung in the balance, where her skills made the end call, she usually dressed down in dark sweaters and jeans topped with the FBI vest. That didn't seem appropriate either.

So, she wore the type of clothes she'd use when she arrived in Rhodes, a traveling outfit that would mark her as a tourist.

Agitated after her quick stop at the office to pick up the file, she drove to the governor's house. Sometimes she hated going into the agency. Lately, the other female agents graced her with cold shoulders and a just-you-dare-to-piss-me-off attitude. Today, they were so sugary sweet, it made her back tighten waiting for the expected shiv.

As shy as she was, she liked most people, just didn't trust everyone. Her pet peeve was unprofessional behavior at work. Not that she didn't enjoy the odd joke or a catching up of the evening-before-session first thing on arrival, but considering the country paid them for eight to twelve hours on some shifts, she felt it only right they spend the better part of the day with their minds on the job.

There were a number of outstanding cases, unfortunate folks with disastrous stories that expected their help, she considered it only right that they serve these people and keep their private shit out of the office.

Don't get her started on the local law enforcement. Maybe it was her particular skillset that pissed off some cops who held her in disdain rather than being relieved when her abilities saved the day. Not that there were too many of those types, thank goodness. But she had to deal with a few buffoons who either hated the fact she was a female or that she could do what they couldn't – take out a dangerous criminal.

Not that she gave a rat's ass about small-minded fools. Those pea-brains didn't count in her world. The only ones who did were fellow law enforcement friends who had the same work code, her large spread-out family, and Bunny.

No boyfriends, not currently. She'd been dating

an ambitious, hot lawyer up until a few months ago who'd caught her eye; that was until he started bitching about her work hours, and how she didn't spend enough time or energy on their relationship. What relationship? Three dinners with him having expectations of bedroom privileges afterward about covered the story of their so-called relationship.

By the time Sophia had left her teens behind, she'd had her fill of the opposite sex and seldom got taken in by their tempting ways and one-track minds. Before she'd graduated, there'd been one occasion where she'd let a sweet talker get past her reserve and had paid for that mistake with weeks of worrying herself sick until her body verified she'd bypassed that particular problem. Never again did she let another person control her choices, both in how much she drank or whatever sex games would follow.

She pulled up to a red light and automatically scanned the area around her. The day had started out cooler than most of the Washington mornings in late May. People were wearing jackets and jeans rather than the usual shorts, which was the official dress code for most of the spring and summer months.

One unshaved, dirty-faced fellow caught her attention. She sensed his interest in the older woman next to him wasn't strictly neighborly. She watched him sidle up beside the parcel-laden senior so he had the best angle to steal her purse.

Gentle Jesus, he was that blatant. Didn't even try to be sneaky. Sophia checked her surroundings and saw why he felt so bold. There weren't many people on the street, and of those few, none were close by. Sophia pulled her car further up the street and stopped. She slid from the driver's side so she could use the cover from the other parked vehicles to get closer. Sure'n there he was now, watching like a cat stalking a bird, giving his prey a few more steps where they'd be in the shadow of an alley that he could shove her into and overwhelm her.

Moving quickly, Sophia got within a few feet. With his attention focused on his victim, he didn't even see her. When he began to make his move, she edged closer and spoke softly so as not to scare him into doing something rash. "Don't you be doing that now, boy-o. It's a bad idea."

He hesitated long enough for the older woman to sense something going on behind her. Just as she would have rushed away, he made his play for her bag. Ripping it off her shoulder, he aimed a blow at the poor overweight soul that Sophia intercepted. Rethinking his plans, he took off like a shot, only to slam into the wall Sophia pushed him into.

Fast as a furious cat protecting her young, Sophia had moves driven by instincts that had shocked her trainers. Always anticipating logical actions by others gave her those few seconds to be ahead of their next move. She'd expected the prick to head for the alley, and he hadn't disappointed her.

She held the skinny male against the bricks while she reclaimed the now furious woman's belongings. "FBI. Don't move, buddy. You know you shouldn't take things that don't belong to you."

"I wasn't doin' nothing."

Suddenly, the victim, feeling safe, decided to take part. Dyed black hair flying around her furious face and chubby arms swinging wildly, the woman clobbered the perp with her recovered purse, hitting at him everywhere but making sure his head got the majority of the blows.

She screamed her rage, her overly painted bright red lips shouting, "You're a lying so and so. You pushed me, you putz." Again, she swung and connected, her face so mottled that Sophia feared for the lady's overworked heart. But she held onto the perp and let the woman at him, keeping the grin off her face.

The guy tried to protect himself and then made the mistake of spewing more lies that made everything worse. "No. I wasn't going to steal it. You dropped it... swear to God!"

"Now you take the Lord's name in vain? Schmuck! Putz! You think I don't know what you were gonna do? My Levi, God bless his sweet soul, is sick in bed and needs this money for his medicine. Which he deserves. 'Cause that man worked hard all his life. Not like you, you lying piece of garbage. You're a bandit. Stealing from old ladies. You should be embarrassed. Your mother would be ashamed she raised such a bum."

Crying, tears of rage pouring over her cheeks, now exhausted and clutching her handbag against her chest, the agitated senior finally ended her tirade, gathered her parcels, and bustled around them.

She aimed a comment at Sophia and a smile, "Thank you sweetheart for helping this old lady."

Sophia, not expecting to make an arrest, didn't have any handcuffs on her. At the moment, she had the wriggling idiot in a hold where he moved and broke his arm or stayed quiet. "Ma'am, please wait. I'll make a call and we can take down your information. Press charges."

"I can't wait. My Levi, God bless his sweet soul, needs his medicine. I'm sorry officer, I have to go." Suddenly, she turned back. When the loser saw her intention, he tried to hide behind Sophia, but she wouldn't let him. He'd take whatever treatment the old lady wanted to dish out, and as far as Sophia was concerned, it wouldn't be even close to what he deserved.

Still bursting with anger, her pink flowered pantsuit all crinkled and misshapen, her parcels gathered messily under her arm, she yelled her final rant, "Farshtunkener! Next time pick on someone your own size. You... you dummkopf!" Her foot shot out, and her kick landed on his shins.

Sophia let him drop to the ground while he clutched his leg and watched her newest hero hurry up the street. The thought popped into her mind that the *dummkopf* had picked on the wrong old lady.

Observing the spirited woman with her head held high, she decided she wanted to be just like her when she grew up. Those few seconds of introspection was all the perp needed to wriggle away from her loosening hold and be gone. A split second of indecision and Sophia stepped down. She knew if she gave chase, she'd most likely have caught the attacker, but then she'd have to make an arrest, wait for back up, and be late for her meeting.

The fact that the guy hadn't succeeded helped her make that choice. She headed for her car and called in what happened, gave them his identification, the location and asked for the uniforms to be on the lookout for the sicko because his desperation would drive him into trying again soon.

Brushing herself down, she resumed her trip and ended at the governor's house just in time for her appointment. She steeled herself to behave, be nice, no matter what awaited her. After all, this woman's children had been taken from her, and in Sophia's estimation, that gave the poor lady a lot of leeway.

Within minutes of their introduction, Sophia's

heart went out to the governor. Observing her swollen eyes and agitated movements, nonetheless, she found that the elegant woman greeted her with dignity. She maintained a calm air and gave Sophia the respect due in her position with the FBI.

Sophia's keen sweep of the room approved of the minimal, tasteful furnishings. The pearl-gray printed wallpaper gave off a soothing effect to whatever stressful situations that might appear for an important government official.

"I'm so sorry about your children being taken, Governor. I know you must be grieving. No doubt, they're missing you terribly. Have you had any contact?"

"Please, call me Maureen. In this situation, I understand we'll be on intimate terms so we can stay in touch."

"Do you have a nickname that your husband doesn't know about, one I can use when I message or call you from Rhodes?"

"My brother calls me sissy. He's the only one who ever used that term. Will that work?"

"Sure, Sissy it is. Has Manos ever heard him refer to you that way?"

"No. He only uses it when we're alone, and he wants to tease."

"Then from now on, I will think of you as Sissy and only refer to you in that way. Now, when did you last talk with Jack or Casey?"

"I spoke with them when they were in the

boarding area to catch the plane. I drove them to the airport but had to say goodbye once they passed through to customs. My husband's mother was dying, and she requested to see her grandchildren before she passed."

"Which you later found out was a lie."

"Yes. But I believed him when he told me. How was I to refuse? I couldn't go with them at the time. Government responsibilities stopped me."

"Which he knew would happen. He'd planned it perfectly."

"Yes, so I know now. I was to follow a few days later."

"That's when they barred you from the airport and made you return home? I'm not being intrusive, but I need to ask. Were you and your husband quarreling? Or had any problems that would drive him to such an action?"

"It's okay, Sophia. I understand it's necessary for you to know what might have led up to him behaving this way. We've been quarreling for some time. Other than our link with the children, he's been difficult – especially lately. He says he's under a lot of stress, and it showed up in his attitude about everything. And... it's been building to where he's been impossible."

"Has this been going on for long?"

"Yes. We lost our way right after the twins were born. Since then, we've basically been acting our roles. My children are my life, Agent Dunne. I can't visualize a future without them in it. It's unbearable."

"Please, call me Sophia. I'm not a mother myself, Governor. Therefore, I can't put myself in your shoes. But I have a strong imagination. Right now, it's telling me that there's no pain worse than how a mother feels to have her children ripped out of her arms. Please know I'll do everything in my power to get Jack and Casey back home where they belong. I've studied the case thoroughly, memorized photos, addresses, and will arrive in Rhodes two days from now."

"You'll keep in touch?"

"As much as possible. I have some relatives I'll have to greet on my arrival... which will remove any suspicions that I might be there on business. Thankfully, my Yaya had a huge group of friends on the island, many in higher circles, and I'm thinking to use those connections to get me close to your husband and his family."

"That's perfect. You've already made me feel hope that will sustain me while you search. Just don't get into any danger. Be careful, Sophia. You are my only hope."

"You say that like you expect there to be a risk."

"My husband can be a very cruel person, and if he's at all threatened, there's no telling what he might do. Especially now that he's feeling safer in his own country."

"Then I'll be extra cautious. Thank you for the

warning."

Sophia got up to leave and was engulfed in warm arms that trembled as they hugged. "Thank you, Sophia. I feel your sympathy, and I know you care. I-I wish I could go with you, but if you need anything, you let... ahh, you let me know."

Chapter Six

Sophia couldn't stop thinking about Maureen Reagan and her warmth. How she greeted her with such self-possession. Although, at the final moment, before she left, she got the feeling that she almost slipped. What was it she said? Oh right, if you need anything, let me know. Why did Sophia get the feeling that she was going to say something else and then changed the words? And, how could 'letting her know about any problems' make a difference when they were in two separate parts of the world?

Strange.

But then again, when you're grieving for your kids, one's mind might be foggy and forgetful. Sophia headed back to her apartment to begin organizing and wasn't surprised to see her boss helping himself to the beer in her fridge,

"You know, when I gave you that key to look after the place last time I was in Greece, I didn't mean for you to make yourself at home anytime you wanted to."

"Yeah – well arrest me, Sophie. I needed to talk with you away from the office."

"Don't call me Sophie. You know I hated it when you and dad started with that nickname. It always meant you'll want me to do something you know I won't want to do."

"Who says you won't want to please your old playmate?"

"Okay, now you're really scaring me. What's up? The straight deal, no prettying up the details."

"You know what, missy, I'm gonna have to speak with Pat about your distrustful attitude. It's not an attractive trait in an old maid."

Laughing now, like she knew he meant for her to do, she settled with her own beer on the sofa next to him, put a quick stranglehold on his neck for a few seconds, and then got serious. "So, what do you need me to know, boy-o, that you came all the way over here to talk about?"

Serious, his face losing the grin, he pulled out a report and handed it over. "There's a shipment of twenty or so kids and young people gathered from mostly eastern European countries stowed away in a container on a cargo ship that sailed out of Amsterdam sometime in the last few days. Problem is, that's all the info we have."

"How do you know for sure?"

"There are anti-human trafficking initiatives starting up in many countries where the problem has grown to ridiculous proportions. Members from different human rights groups gather information by hanging out in places where the traffickers tend to gather. Sometimes, they get lucky and a blabbermouth is heard bragging. Bars in Amsterdam where they openly smoke weed that loosens inhibitions have been a virtual dumpster for intelligence. Once the data is confirmed, they share it with us."

Sophia took a sip of her beer before she asked, "They couldn't be more specific?"

"I wish they were, but this time, they only found out after the fact." He pointed at the file she held and added, "We have a list of all those freighters, but who knows which one is carrying our container. Look, if there's any way you can track this info from Manos in time for us to be able to intercept that vessel, it would be a bonus."

Bruner couldn't help seeing the willingness on her face and added, "I don't want you to take any risks, Sophie."

"It's not that, boss. It's the thought of that number of people being locked in a regular-size container for all those days at sea. Can you imagine what their circumstances would be like? My God, that's barbaric. What if someone gets sick, or fights break out? Isn't there any way you can search all incoming ships?"

"Do you know how many of those suckers arrive each day? And how much manpower it would take, not to mention breaking laws by forcing our way onboard without warrants? It's unthinkable. Unless we know the exact ship or get a lead on who's involved in the felony, our hands are tied."

"What do you want me to do? How can I help?"

"Look, we know that Manos is involved in this slavery scheme so we're hoping he might have the information we need to find that container. From what we can tell, you'll have about a week before they make port. Just keep your eyes and ears open for any indication that might involve this situation."

She nodded and added, "Gentle Jesus, Bunny. I can't take any chances with the children's safety. If I'm able to get them away from their father and sneak them off the island, I'll need all my wits about me. Our plan to steal them away on one of the daily cruises to Turkey, and from there, fly them home can work, but I need to stay under the radar as much as possible. Play the bereaved granddaughter coming home to accept her inheritance. Not snooping around for information."

"That's exactly true. But I also know you. Somehow, young lady, you have a way of being able to do things others can't. I'm just leaving you with this report that you'll memorize and then destroy. And... if you can find out anything at all pertaining to these circumstances, you will let me know, and I'll do the work here to follow up on it, okay?"

Sophia nodded. She'd already set up lines of connections she fully intended to take advantage of once she arrived in Rhodes. Her grandmother was friends with many of the older families. They were the wealthier folks on the island, and she intended to use every avenue she could to instigate her way as quickly as possible into the same circle as Manos Savas. The faster she got those kids back to their mother, the better off everyone would be.

Chapter Seven

Maureen waited for the door to close behind Sophia before she joined Sam in the other room. He remained sitting at the desk, staring at the monitor, looking dazed.

She waited for him to speak. When he didn't, she began, "What do you think? Were you as shocked as I was that the FBI is sending a woman agent?"

His amazed glare cut her way. "Truthfully, it never dawned on me. When she stepped into the room, I'll admit to being floored. But they wouldn't be sending anyone they didn't trust to be able to handle this assignment, you know that, Sissy."

"Yes. In fact, I liked her immediately. By the time she left, I felt better. Somehow, she gave me faith that this scheme will work. She came across as a person comfortable with her own abilities. And... we both know my annoying spouse loves the ladies. That's never been in doubt."

"Well, if it's any solace, I've just run a background check on the woman, and she's one of the top agents around here, efficient and follows protocol. Very highly thought of and takes on a lot of the tougher cases. You can relax, sis. That silver-haired chick will do a good job."

***

Sam hadn't shared everything he'd learned in Google about Special Agent Sophia Dunne. About her sharpshooter trophies won at FBI tournaments from all over the country, and how she was known to take shots others would never try.

The fact she hardly ever aimed to kill – just the opposite – put her in a category few others ever reached. She'd wound her victims whenever possible and was commended for those abilities. The reporter had disclosed only two cases where she'd gone all the way. Both involved hardened killers. Once, when a baby's life hung in the balance. The other, a twelve-year-old who'd been brutalized and faced imminent death by his stepfather if she didn't take the kill shot. According to the story, she hadn't hesitated.

Reading the continuous comments about a female hero who anyone would hold in high esteem made him count his blessings that she'd appeared in the picture at a time when they needed her most.

Sam couldn't come out in the open in Rhodes as himself. Any impersonation he adopted might work, providing he didn't meet up with Manos. His brother-in-law would recognize him immediately and be forced to make the kids disappear yet again.

The fact that Manos held them in his villa on the Greek island where he came from was a bonus. He obviously felt safe having them there with him, protected by his government, and no doubt, scads of security.

Sam understood the need to keep a low profile, stay off the radar and let Agent Sophia work in the open. And as long as they knew where the children were, and they had a good chance to recover them, he'd behave.

But he also knew if they didn't return those two kids to their grieving mother soon, Maureen would fade away before his very eyes. Always fragile, but only when it came to her family. The woman had the hide of a rhino over politics, the voice of a lion when she stood up for other's rights, but the delicate heart of a vulnerable woman for those she loved. And she adored her babies.

***

Maureen had never seen Sam bemused before, not like this. His stunned expression worried her until he spoke and admitted he liked the agent and had already begun delving into her background – nothing she hadn't expected from her efficient brother.

That he'd confirmed Sophia's career background didn't surprise her. Knowing her brother's demand for excellence, she'd expected no less. And his acceptance was exactly what she needed to verify her own opinion.

However, the dazed look on his face came as a shock. Not bragging, her brother turned most every woman's head he encountered. Which she never did understand. It wasn't like he was movie-star handsome. His stature, not overly tall, was strong but not with Schwarzenegger-like muscles. In fact, his medium height didn't intimidate or present a menacing figure to those he stood against until they tried to take him on.

Nevertheless, he had a charisma about him that caught a woman's attention. Once they looked into his smiling brown eyes and caught the seductive vibe he'd perfected, they'd invariably fold and become sucked into his special attraction. Wavy hair, black with silvery strands, cut short in a military-style always managed to look sexy and windblown. His self-possessed manner gave everyone the feeling he'd protect them no matter what, and his cheeky smile drew in even the most impervious.

For her, it was his heart, his big beautiful heart he kept hidden away from the world that was his best feature. She never did understand what had bruised that organ. Something happened when he'd been younger, something he'd never shared, but from the time he'd been in his early twenties, he'd changed. A brittle shield had formed, and he'd closed off that sweet portion which she'd loved the most.

Still, he was her big brother, the man she admired above all others and relied on more than anyone else alive. Sure, she'd lost the pal of her youth, and she missed that person terribly. But, when it came to depending on someone to get back her children, her big brother Sam would be her first choice.

As the head of the Reagan Group, who held the respect and command over so many other specialists in that arena, he was sought after by governments and major companies all over the globe.

She was blessed. She knew it. It's what kept her from going completely insane.

Chapter Eight

Sophia's arrival at the Rhodes airport was bittersweet. Every other time she'd come to visit, Yaya would be waiting for her. On this occasion, her cousin, Barney, stood with a long face and sad eyes. Normally, she'd have arrived without any fanfare and taken a few days to adjust to her new circumstances as a bereaved granddaughter, but she didn't have the luxury of time.

She approached with her arms open. "Hi, Cuz. Thanks for meeting me."

His bearing was that of a man who's shoulders carried more weight than they should. Considering he had five children all under the age of seven, she understood his manner and even commiserated. She loved children, that was always a given, but having so many all arriving around the same time would be a heavy burden for anyone. Thankfully, his wife Ellie carried most of the brunt, leaving Barney free to run his classy beach spa hotel.

"Of course, I came to get you. It's a sad time for us without Yaya. We wanted you to know we'd be happy for you to stay with us rather than at her house all by yourself. I don't want you to be alone and grieving for her."

"And yet, that's exactly what I need to do, Barney. You know that as well as I do. I want to say my goodbyes. I'll come over to your place soon. Just give me today to settle in."

"Fine. But Ellie would cut me into small pieces if I didn't offer you a room with us." His sincerity rang true.

She grinned. Her six-foot-two, thickset cousin feared the wrath of his five-foot-two skinny wife. "You've already organized a cocktail party for me so I can say hello to all the family at once rather than having to reach out to each of them separately. That's a huge help, Barney. Today, later, I need to visit Old Town and hit the favorite places where Yaya and I always headed for."

"Don't forget, while you're there, please stop and say hello to Yanis. He's asked about you more than once. You know he's got the gift. I think he's worried about you, at least I get that feeling. So, unless you want him stalking you, stop over at his fish spa and see him."

"Of course, I will. How is he doing?"

"He's fine but frets about his favorites. You've

been one since you were a small girl."

Sophia laughed. "Was it me or my mother he had eyes for? He'd light up every time we were together."

"They went to the same school. Who knows, maybe they were romantically involved. I've never asked him."

"Maybe one day I will. Here's the house, Barney. Thank you for making sure the flowers were all taken care of since Julie left. The place looks wonderful." Sophia feasted her eyes on the golden house with vine-covered balconies streaming with the same pink and purple bougainvillea her Yaya had always grown. It made her heart ache. Yet she felt better than she would have if the place looked deserted and unkempt.

Barney pulled into the driveway and got out of the car to retrieve her suitcases. "Are you sure I can't come in with you? I can fetch you your favorite tea and hold your hand."

"No, I'll be fine. You know I dislike anyone seeing me upset. I'm an ugly crier, so it's best if I get it over with while there're no witnesses. I'll come to you soon, I promise. This morning, what's left of it, I'll hang with Yaya's spirit."

Within a few minutes, Sophia had her suitcases in her room, and she stood at the entrance to her grandmother's den where the older woman had spent most of her time. The well-used easy chair looked as if her Yaya had just gotten up to leave the room for a few minutes and would return.

She sat down, closed her eyes, and let the memories flood along with the accompanying tears. She'd loved that woman so much. They'd had a rapport she'd never felt with another. No one else had treated her quite the same or understood her better.

Her Yaya knew her secrets, about the days when she'd been forced to come to terms with a threat that would have changed her future. And how the relief of not being pregnant had made her feel guilt that had never quite disappeared.

She'd helped her accept her vulnerability towards a certain type of male, the seduction they might use to overcome any woman's boundaries, and how to see it clearly for what it was. Not a weakness of her character, but a normal female inclination to that sort of charm.

The Greek beauty had also been the one to teach her how to shoot. Oh, they'd trained her in Quantico, sure. But it was her grandmother who'd schooled her miracle, the sharp eye and hand coordination that made her special. She'd taught her the lesson of how to see clearly as she looked through the rifle's telescope – to judge distances and react quickly.

Sitting there in her Yaya's home, she ached with love and the pain of loss. Until she imagined a voice in her head that she'd yearned to hear.

"Éla, come, my child. Don't sit there missing me. Get

up! Go! See the people who make you happy. For as long as you remember me, I will be with you."

Knowing her Yaya would expect no less, she wiped her tears and changed into a filmy, long, white eyelet creation – her grandmother's favorite of her dresses she often wore while staying in Rhodes – and headed to the best part of the Island. Always sunny here during the spring and summer, the heat of the Mediterranean sun soothed her and put a spring in her step.

The Old City of Rhodes (Old Town), surrounded by medieval castle walls with seven gates, housed The Palace of the Grandmaster and was the most impressive site of all the Greek islands. A world of tourist shops, restaurants, bars, and museums, more like a Turkish bazaar than any other Greek city, resided within its thick parapets. Anyone with imagination would be touched by the history of the place, imagining the past where knights ruled, and armies battled.

Today, it's magic still existed as a tourist haven where folks came to spend their vacations among kind-hearted Greek hosts. Sightseeing, eating wonderful Greek dishes at the various restaurants, shopping to their heart's content, and constantly surrounded by the gorgeous blues of the Mediterranean ocean made it a holiday retreat like no other.

But then, Sophia was biased. Once inside the primitive walls, she headed for her favorite restaurant where they greeted her with affectionate hugs and commiserated with her on the passing of her Yaya. Soon, without her having to place an order, they'd set her up at the front table with all her favorites.

Lynia, her special friend who's family owned the place and who'd worked at the same open-air bistro since she could remember, left her to greet other guests. While she soaked up the sunshine, enjoying her favorite Ouzomezes, appetizers they served with a glass of their finest Ouzo saved for special guests, she waited for the main course of traditional Moussaka, the best in the city.

Surveying her surroundings, she slowly planned her options for the next few days. Suddenly, a ruckus began in the restaurant across from where she sat. Separated by only a few feet, she listened to the accents of what she decided were a group of happy Canadians newly arrived.

She smiled as the four excited tourists ordered fancy cocktails that had flags of the various countries attached to slices of fruit that decorated large goblet-styled glasses. Some of the fancy glasses were huge, and she waited for them to ask the price before going ahead and placing their order.

When that didn't happen, she knew what their bill would be and the shock that would follow. Silly tourists, enthusiastic from their arrival in this heavenly place, hadn't yet learned the valuable lesson of setting a price before ordering a treat.

Sure enough, as they happily enjoyed their fancy drinks, their glee for having arrived in paradise became obvious, and Sophia felt her sympathy take shape. Finished and ready to move on, they were given the final bill, and that's when the blow of finding the price of their entertainment to be outrageous, they revealed their shock. Only one, a frizzy-haired, older, argumentative woman, questioned the waiter angrily.

"Seriously? You expect us all to pay twenty-five euros? For each drink? It's outrageous... ridiculous."

Sophia knew she shouldn't interfere. It wasn't done, but how could she sit by and watch her father's countrymen be cheated so badly.

She stepped over to where the bar's owner stood, a smirk on his face as he watched yet another group of people being robbed. When he saw her, at first, he lit up with greeting until he noticed the disgust on her face. "Henri, you either discount their drinks, or I'll make such a fuss, they'll be talking about it for days."

A whistle from Henri caught the waiter's eye. A shake of Henri's head made it known for the waiter to step down and be reasonable. A friend of the confrontational woman had seen Sophia's approach and seemed to know she'd made the difference. The lovely, short-haired woman nodded her way, a thank you for sure.

Once the final bill had been settled, the still angry woman picked up the empty goblet-styled glass and stuck it under her arm. "Even at half price, the cost is pure highway robbery. I'll be taking the glass too. Though I still feel cheated, it will remind me to check the prices first."

Off she trotted, her party amazed at her cheek, yet willing to take her side, laughed at her brazen behavior and no doubt feeling better about the whole situation. Especially when the waiter stood down and said nothing.

Sophia returned to her table to find she had a guest relaxing in the chair opposite from hers. His handsome face took her breath away. A well-trimmed beard and mustache, plus aviator-style sunglasses hid most of his face, yet she felt an instant attraction.

He was the exact type of male she'd learned to stay away from. The sort who attracted her, spun her senses and in the past had made her behave like a sappy female rather than a strong, modern woman.

"I'm sorry. You've taken my table. I only stood up for a minute to say hello to an old friend."

The cheeky bastard looked at the empty plates and glass and then glanced to the ground as if searching for something. Finally, he said, "No name that I can find. The rest of the tables are full." He grinned with a sly kind of a smile that had her catch her breath, waved his hand at her chair, and spoke softly, "I'm more than happy to share this one... Sophia."

Chapter Nine

Sam had been watching Sophia from a restaurant on the opposite corner. He'd been waiting for her to enter the old town area and knew she'd most likely come through the gate closest to her grandmother's house.

He'd arrived in Rhodes the day before, spending every minute investigating and familiarizing himself with the place. Since it was his first time in Rhodes, he was annoyed he had to work rather than vacation like the rest of the lucky folks wandering around happily immersed in their historical surroundings. Instead he spent his time making plans on how he would meet up with his so-called partner.

Forced to ignore the many wonderful sightseeing possibilities, he stuck with the tactic he'd chosen and made up his mind they would meet asap. His brilliant and snoopy computer genius, John-john had informed him of Sophia's love of this specific restaurant and how she'd most likely be showing up sometime on her first day.

Planning the hours of her arrival, the time it would take her to settle in and hopefully wander to the market, he'd only had an hour's wait before she'd appeared.

Not expecting the beauty who'd arrived wearing a pretty, flowy white dress and sparkly sandals, he'd watched for the same agent he'd last seen in black pants and leather jacket. The shock of her appearance hit him hard.

Agent Sophia had been stunning as his sister's guest, but in these surroundings, she shone. The constant gentle breeze that gave one respite from the heat of the sun floated her white hair that gleamed like fine silk. And her carriage – walking tall, straight-backed, and smiling nostalgically made him see a woman who had faith in her abilities and liked herself.

His solar plexus took a beating from the tightened muscles. If allowed, this female could be his nirvana. There were very few times in his life where he wanted nothing to do with his business, his world, his responsibilities, but this young woman could be the catalyst for him to give it all up and lose himself.

Tempted, but knowing the stakes were too high to mess up, he forced his interest back to the job and watched for a chance, a way to introduce himself to her without there being any suspicions.

Delighted when it became so easy, he observed her interference with a wrongdoing and cheered her on for helping some unfortunate tourists being taken advantage of.

He'd seen this sort of thing often in the many terribly disgusting poor countries where he'd worked, places unlike Rhodes. Completely opposite of the mind-blowing beauty seen here. Where the wonderful Mediterranean colors, incredible smells, pretty tourists, and wonderful shops battled for prominence in the colorful, cheerful marketplace. He'd fallen in love with everything in the city and wished he could leave his life for a month, rent an Airbnb and stay put.

When Sophia finally returned to her table and approached him, she wore an obstinate glare for his impudence. All he wanted to do was pick her up in his arms, swing her around crazily and spend the next few days getting to know the woman under the mask she'd quickly assumed.

Instead, he played the part of the lothario vacationer who had nothing to do but flirt with pretty ladies. He'd even dressed the role, wearing summer-weight well-fitting slacks and a short-sleeved navy T-shirt that showed off the military tattoos on his arms and the tan he'd acquired during his on-going assignment in Tehran. All he needed now was for her to believe his story. That his last three tours overseas had done a number on him that forced a well-deserved recuperation.

Convincing her would take some acting on his part, but wasn't that exactly what he did for a living? Pretend to be someone he wasn't. Taking on the hard-assed shell of a man who cared about nothing and no one when in fact, he had more principles than most and a bigger heart than many.

His problem wasn't having the woman take him seriously, it was him taking himself seriously. She was nothing like the usual hardened female he encountered out in the world while doing his job. Females who knew the rules had erased their femininity and wanted the same from a man that he'd want from them. A night of kindness and a shared bed.

Agent Sophia had nothing in common with them. Sam didn't like breaking hearts, but if it meant getting Casey and Jack home to his sister, he would do whatever it took.

Chapter Ten

How the hell did he know her name? Sophia recognized the flirter for what he was, and she didn't like having to deal with him, especially now. But in her mind, she only had a few choices.

Push the situation where Lynia would show up and take over, dealing with the handsome customer in her own magical way – making another table instantly appear where she would place him.

Or... as he suggested, she could join him and get the answer to the mystery of how he knew her name. She'd really wanted more time alone to be in her favorite place, but he'd spoiled that now anyway.

Maddened by the impudence of the man, she tried to stare him down without speaking and watched as his grin widened. He lowered his sunglasses slightly, winked at her and added, "I really don't bite. Sit." Then he leaned over to pull her chair back even further. It was the last word spoken softly that convinced her.

"Please."

She sat.

Miraculously, as if she'd waited just for this moment, Lynia came to the table with a full tray of grapes, olives with dip, and chocolate-covered strawberries. She removed Sophia's used dishes and placed another glass of ouzo in front of both people now seated.

"Sophia, another of your favorites. And you, sir, please accept our welcome to Rhodes drink. Can I bring you a menu? Anything?"

The man smiled graciously and thanked Lynia, saying he'd stopped for a happy-hour drink and would appreciate a beer in one of those smaller boots he'd seen others being served in. He asked Sophia if she'd like a cocktail or any other drink. Before she could refuse, Lynia patted her hand and said, "No problem. I know exactly what drink she likes the most. One sex-on-the-beach coming up. We make it especially for her here."

Knowing she should have told Lynia she didn't want anything else, that she'd be having to sip her third ouzo carefully if she wanted to get home safely, she said nothing. Her friend worked hard to make a living until the tourist season started in the summer months and the cruise ships docked daily, so every penny earned now kept them afloat.

As soon as they were alone, Sophia asked the question she'd held on the tip of her tongue. "How do you know my name?"

He pointed at the nearby shop. "I was looking at those shirts hanging there behind those tables, and I heard a woman exclaim when she saw you... Sophia Dunne. She seemed delighted you were here and had no doubt been waiting for a moment to catch your eye and attack."

Sophia turned in the direction he gestured and sure enough, there sat one of her childhood friends along with three other people she knew. As soon as she'd turned their way, the attractive blonde acknowledged her and stood to approach.

"Sophia! Hello. I'm so glad you're here. Barney said he expected you any day." They hugged affectionately, and Sophia saw the interest her girlfriend had in her companion. Wishing she could ignore the blatant unspoken suggestion that they be presented, she turned instead to make an introduction. "This is one of my childhood friends, Corinne Floros." Suddenly, she realized her pickle. She had no idea what this man's name was. Understanding her dilemma, her relaxed, smiling companion didn't miss a beat.

"So nice to meet you. I'm a new friend of Sophia's, just arrived in Rhodes, Sam Mattas. Would you like to join us? If you prefer privacy, I can make myself scarce." He feared Sophia would take him up on the idea. He knew the circumstances of her trip and about her grandmother's passing and didn't have the meanness in him to refuse her this time with a friend.

Before Sophia could agree, Corinne's laugh rang out, and she graciously answered, "Of course you're not to leave. Now that she's home, Sophia and I will have plenty of time to catch up soon."

Lynia arrived just then with their drinks, and Sam not only paid the bill but asked Corinne if she would like anything.

"No, I can't stay. But thank you. You're very kind." She reached over and took Sophia's hand. "Did Barney tell you we're having a big birthday barbecue at the olive farm for Auntie on Saturday? You must come. She'll be distressed if you're not there, especially now she knows you're in Rhodes. She misses your Yaya so much she'll like having someone she can talk with about her friend."

Sophia had no idea there was a gathering. Sipping her favorite drink, she shook her head, and it made her slightly woozy. "Barney must have forgotten to tell me. But, of course, I'll be there."

"Great! Oh sorry, the rest of the group are waiting for me. I'll call, and we can make arrangements. Bring Sam if you like. It's a casual get-together."

Ignoring Corinne's flirty goodbye smile for Sam, slightly annoyed at her friend's obviousness, Sophia took another long sip of the delicious fruity concoction and changed the subject. "Will the rest of your family be there?"

"Yes, the whole bunch of them. Even Ellie's cousin, Manos Savas, who is here with his children for the summer. He's promised to bring the little ones. I haven't seen them since they were babies."

Attentive, but not wanting to appear so, she lifted her glass to finish her drink and chuckled, "Goodness, it has been a long while for the whole family to be together. I look forward to catching up with everyone."

Sophia waved her friend off and turned in time to catch the interest that appeared on her companion's face before he lowered his sunglasses.

Uncomfortable, not really wanting to be with this stranger, she took some euros from her pocket, laid them on the bill tray and made to rise. Before she could take one step, the handsome jerk added, "What time would you like me to pick you up for the party?"

Chapter Eleven

Sam knew he couldn't actually go to the barbecue, but he liked yanking Sophia's chain. And, she didn't disappoint.

"I'm sorry. Did you say you would pick me up for the barbecue? Yes, well that's not going to happen. You see, number one, I don't know you. And number two, it's for family members only." Incensed, Sophia picked up her still full shot-glass with the last of the ouzo and downed the contents, slamming the glass down to make a point. Then she gathered her belongings.

Before she could stand, he spoke, "Okay. It's my turn, and I'll take number three. It's simple really. I was invited. You're my witness, you heard Corinne."

The cheek of the bastard! Sophia couldn't believe he was seriously pushing to go where he wasn't wanted. She stood and leaned over, her many necklaces dangling in front. Before he could stop her, she whipped off his sunglasses and dropped them on the table, and then she leaned close enough so he could see how serious she was.

"Look, I didn't invite you to this table, and I sure as hell am not going to invite you to my family's barbecue. So back off."

That's when her foot slid out from under her, and she would have fallen across the table without his speed in using his arms to support her so she could sit instead.

***

Gentle Jesus. She was sloshed. The three ouzos plus the cocktail had gotten to her. Spinning skies, a stomach ready to upchuck and the muggy brainwaves let her know she'd overdone her limit. *Son of a bitch!* And it had to happen in front of the last person she'd ever choose to witness her disgrace.

She slumped in her chair and held her face in her hands until the queasy sensations settled. He spoke low, his raspy male voice casting a spell. "I have my bike right here. If you like, I can get you home before you fall down."

She looked at him and saw his seriousness. He wasn't teasing or wanting to cause her embarrassment.

Lynia suddenly appeared at her side. "Sophia, look at you. I'm so sorry. I should have known better than to serve you so many drinks after you said you'd flown most of the night and hadn't had much time to rest before coming here. Look, my friend, I can get you a taxi to pick you up at Liberty gate, and I'll help you get there if you wish."

Sam interrupted and asked, "Could she ride on my bike with me?" He pointed to the black sleek scrambler parked at the side of the building.

Lynia looked over at the shiny, new vehicle and grinned. "Sophia can handle any kind of motorcycle ever made."

Sophia, not willing to be treated like a baby and having them talk over her head, giggled and added, "Thatsh true. I can ride any bike, anytime. Jush... lead me to it."

In her muddled brain, Sophia knew she'd regret this day. But feeling the way she did, the sooner she got back home, the sooner she could sleep this inebriation off and forget the embarrassment ever happened. Plus, this man irked the hell out of her, and for some dumb, drunken reason, she wanted to prove something to him. What that was, she had no idea.

***

Thankful that they allowed motorcycles of a certain type into the marketplace; Sam had rented his expecting to need transportation. He just never figured it would be to take a drunken Sophia home on the first day. Go figure, their initial meeting would lead to this.

Lynia, helping settle Sophia behind him, gave

him directions to her grandmother's house which was thankfully close by. He swiveled to check on her safety and asked, "You holding on, sweetheart? I'll take it easy, but I don't want to lose you in the traffic."

Laughing as if he'd made the funniest joke, she put her arms around his middle and leaned her cheek against his back. "Jush don't take too many wild turns." And then as if her sense of humor had suddenly revived, she added, "My tummy is slightly queasy. We wouldn't want any accidents, right?"

"I'll drive as if I have my ninety-year-old granny behind me, honey. Just hold on. And I mean that literally."

He started up the motor and circled the square to head in the nearest direction toward her place. There were many similar bikes going back and forth, so the vacationers gave him ample leeway. Easing the machine through the people traffic had him pacing the bike to a low speed, but once they passed through the gate and hit the main thoroughfare, she yelled from behind, "Take the ocean route. It's longer, but itsch beautiful."

There'd be no argument from him. He'd done his homework already by driving on all the various routes, familiarizing himself with the city. He knew exactly how to get to her house and the most panoramic view they could follow on their way. With her arms holding tightly, her chest plowing into his back, and her mouth very near his neck, he decided he never wanted the trip to end.

Her perfume wafted between them, a flowery southern scent like those he remembered from when he bought his sister a gift from Hawaii. He loved their island fragrances, and his head spun from being so close to that magical aroma.

She spoke loudly, her voice carrying, "This is a shpechial view, one of my favorites on the island. Look at that sunset! Sometimes, I dream of this exact vision when I'm back at work."

Appearing like a huge golden circle of flames, weaving streaks of orange, purple, red, and faded blues altogether as a last-ditch effort of beauty, the sun gathered its various hues and slowly began to slither behind the horizon.

"It is beautiful." He yelled his reply and hoped she heard him. But she'd nestled her head against his back now and her arms felt slightly lax. He needed to get her home before she fell off. God, he wished she weren't intoxicated. He'd have given anything to just ride toward that sunset and spend hours on a lone beach getting to know her.

Still heading in the direction she'd suggested, they traveled along the highway when her skirts loosened from under her weight and began flapping wildly around them. As if she'd been suddenly attacked by the overwhelming pleasure of being on a ride, she lifted her arms to the sky, extended her legs wide, and yelled with glee, "I'm here, Yaya. I'm home."

"Hey, little girl, behave. I don't want to lose you." He slowed the bike and shouted at her, not wanting to curb her enthusiasm but fearful of her steadiness.

She laughed, a delightfully happy laugh but did as she was told. Gathering her skirts, she sat on the material, leaving a lot of her legs bare. Taking in the spectacle, he couldn't help but notice that one of her pretty sandals was missing.

This girl, the one clinging to him, her warm body making his hard and needy, would be in his world for the foreseeable future. Thank the good Lord for small mercies. Even if they wouldn't be a couple, unknown to her, they would be working together.

For the first time in... forever, he wanted it to not be about a job. Sam didn't know how much more he could take of his lustful yearnings to be just a guy with his girl, so he shut it down and headed the bike in the direction of Yaya's house. He eased it into the driveway beside the back door.

Once they'd left the beach, she seemed to have slipped into a trance, just holding him quietly. Not paying attention to where they were, she moaned with disapproval on seeing her home. "No. I don't want to be here. It's too sad. I want to keep riding. I love the bike." She pouted and his initial response was to kiss the pout off her mouth and carry her into the house so he could take things even further.

This sweetheart tempted him beyond anything he'd ever been up against before. "I'll take you for a ride another time, sweetie, but now, I'm being a gentleman. You need your bed, Sophia." He slipped off from in front of her and made as if to help her to dismount.

"Wait, take my key and open the door for me, okay?"

Without any hesitation, he took the key and slipped under the vine-covered walkway to the door. That's when he heard the bike start up, and the last thing he saw were her skirts flying behind her as she headed in the direction they just came from, leaving him here all alone.

Slightly pissed, he couldn't help but grin at her devilishness. It was exactly the kind of thing he'd do himself in her place, and so he got it. Knew she needed this time. He only prayed the fresh air had cleared away some of her foggy brain and she wouldn't go too far.

He let himself into the house, into the kitchen area and headed for the coffee machine. He'd think about her possibly connecting with his niece and nephew in a few days and start making plans to assist her if she needed him. He'd be there, just not in the open. In fact, he couldn't do anything with her in the open. And for the first time in a really long time, he wanted to.

Fuck!

He grinned wryly. She'd just dumped him.

He should be furious.

He wasn't.

He couldn't wait to see what her excuse would be.

What a woman!

Chapter Twelve

Sophia sobered up quickly after her unexpected release of inhibitions. The earlier expression of happiness, an action she'd often performed as a teenager overcome with too much emotion, had only been shared with one other person. It was the kind of thing she'd done as a young girl on her bike rides with Yaya. Besieged with the freedom and joy of the experience, she wouldn't be able to contain herself.

Having the same reaction while holding onto a man who she'd just met had thrown her into turmoil. Her brain had cleared long enough for her to know she could be in big trouble. There was something about this guy. Instinctively, she'd known in her heart that if Yaya had been alive today, she'd have liked him. How the hell that seemed so clear had her questioning her sanity.

Rather than taking chances of spending time

alone with him, especially in the mood she'd found herself in, she'd chosen instead to put distance between them. Take this time for herself to reflect and sort out her next couple of days. She had a job to do and nothing could stand in the way of her getting those two kids back to their mother. She'd promised.

Driving onto a public beach parking area on Akti Miaouli Street, the main road across from the Mitsis Grand super expensive hotel, Sophia parked and sat on the bike, her skirts all tucked up and her leg resting against the handlebars. She watched the turquoise water darken and the lighter clouds around the glowing moon weave magic as it began its performance of a spectacular show for the day's end.

She'd come here often as a young girl and watch her favorite scene, thanking God for giving her the wonderful life he'd allowed her to live. Her large family back in Canada, her ties to her father's home in Newfoundland, plus her mother's people here in Rhodes. She counted her blessings the same way she did every time she returned.

Suddenly, she heard something that took her completely away from her happy, slightly drunken musings. Sobs from someone nearby had caught at her heartstrings, and she couldn't ignore the distressing sounds of sadness.

Leaving her motorbike, removing her one sandal, she wandered further along the sandy drifts where they had stacked up many of the day's beach chairs and umbrellas. Following the whimpers of a young person in despair, she finally made out the figure of a slight female curled up on one of the loungers, crying her heart out.

Chapter Thirteen

Sophia would have passed by if the person in such despair happened to be her age or older. After all, at some time or another, everyone had reasons for a breakdown and a need for privacy.

But having no doubts that from the sounds and size of the crier it was a very young girl, she couldn't ignore the problem. What if whoever experienced such wretchedness had serious troubles and needed help? She didn't have it in her to just ignore the obvious.

Instead, she approached slowly so as not to startle the girl and sat near her in the seat across. When the person sensed her sanctuary had been breached, she swiftly arched away in panic.

"It's okay. Don't be scared. I won't hurt you," Sophia spoke soothingly. She showed her hands to prove she was telling the truth, and using her training, gave the other enough space so as not to be invasive.

When she glanced up, Sophia saw her clearly. She looked like a Russian girl who worked in the FBI office back home, same shaped face and blonde hair. One difference was a black mole she had on the lower side of her left cheek. From her appearance, Sophia decided she probably came from somewhere in Eastern Europe. Sophia felt certain she wasn't Greek.

Speaking softly, Sophia began a conversation. "I don't want to intrude, honey, but I had the feeling it's possible you need help. Hearing your cries, I couldn't ignore that you might be in trouble."

The girl swiped at her eyes, only to have them filling again. "You should not be here." Her accent was strong, yet she spoke English. Appearing dumbfounded that anyone would approach and question her, she looked around behind Sophia as if she expected to see others there too.

If suspicion of a stranger's interest had been her only reaction, Sophia might have left her to her sorrow. But this girl's eyes were dilated with fear, and Sophia could smell her anxiety – it was that potent. Looking like a cornered animal, the youngster swiveled in the other direction to be sure no one else approached from that side either.

Another thing that blew Sophia's mind was the drenched outfit the girl wore. The smudged mascara, low-cut top and tight skirt screamed hooker, and yet the wearer couldn't have been more than fifteen... if that. It also appeared as if she'd taken a swim without disrobing.

Sophia had no idea what a kid was doing out on the beach in soggy clothes, crying her heart out, but she knew enough for her cop's instincts to kick in big time. This kid was terrified, and Sophia had no intention of walking away.

"What's wrong, sweetheart? Are you in trouble? My name is Sophia Dunne. Can I help?"

The girl rose and as if it used too much energy, she slumped back, her hands flapping around her as if she didn't know what to say. Her thin strap slipped off her shoulder, which gave her the appearance of a child playing dress-up.

Maybe she didn't understand English. Sophia asked her, "Do you know what I'm saying?"

Nodding, yet still not answering, she broke down yet again as if her heart would break. Sophia, unable to stop herself, moved in next to her and put her arms around the girl. "Tell me. I can help you. What's your name?"

Broken spirit, her words strongly accented, she said, "Anastasia. Stasia." More tears followed. "I'm big fool. I can't do what they ask. I want to kill myself. I try, but I can swim." At this point she wailed her words, making Sophia listen closely. "I save myself. Yet, I want to die. I need to die... because they won't let me go."

The last words were hysterical and so full of anguish that Sophia felt the tremors from the girl's body enter her own. Anxiety, like what she sensed from her companion, crushed everything else from her mind. What was this all about? Gentle Jesus, this poor immigrant girl's mutterings scared her, because she had an inkling of what she'd stumbled on to.

The human trafficking around the globe didn't have a free pass in Greece. In fact, from her research she knew they had thousands being brought here every year to fill the menial, low-paying jobs the Greeks refused to do themselves. Every city needed the poor young people from uncaring countries willing to perform in unthinkable ways.

As soon as she'd seen her outfit, Sophia guessed what they'd set this kid up for. It wasn't housework or a low-paid job. Everything inside her screamed *no fucking way*. This would not happen, not here, not tonight, not ever if she had her way.

"Come with me. We'll get you out of here. Where you'll be safe."

Studying her character, the girl stared into Sophia's face. Sophia held her stare, showing the kid she meant every word. Stasia nodded and started to stand. Something made her look over Sophia's shoulder. Whatever she saw filled her face with horror.

Chapter
Fourteen

Two large men were approaching at a run, their black suits making it hard to see them in the dark. It was their faces that showed in the moonlight, and the grim looks they wore let Sophia know they weren't happy to see her with the girl.

Too bloody bad. She grabbed the girl's hand and pulled her to her feet, running away from their pursuers in the opposite direction. "Come. Quickly. We can get away."

Obviously terrified, the girl followed, but she warned, her breath catching. "They have guns. You run. If I go back, they don't shoot me." As if overcome by her own words, she tried to pull her hand from Sophia's grasp, but Sophia wouldn't allow it.

"No. We'll both run. Hurry. On the street. I have a bike."

Suddenly, a third man joined the chase, and he

was much closer. He cut them off and forced Sophia to stop. She pushed Stasia away from her and turned to meet him. He slowed, coming at her with a strange grin on his face. He seemed to be enjoying the fact that she intended to stand up to him.

His voice was rough with conviction. "The girl. She's with me."

Sophia saw the other two stop to catch their breath, as if they expected buddy here to look after things. Good! She didn't want to have to fight them all, but she would if forced to. "Yet she doesn't want to be with you, does she?"

First, he looked at the girl who stood trembling to the side of them and gave her an order. "Stasia, go back to the hotel. You won't be punished if you do as I tell you."

"Will you leave this lady alone?"

"Of course. Once you're across the street, I'll walk away."

Anastasia started in the direction of the hotel; her last words were for Sophia. "Thank you for caring."

Once Stasia had put a good distance between them, he rushed Sophia, his fist just catching the side of her face. Slipping, as if losing her balance in the sand, she sneakily gathered a handful of it and waited to see the prick's next move.

Sophia didn't take her eyes off the assailant. Instead, she moved toward him so quickly, he didn't expect her attack. Using the handful of sand she'd gathered while his attention had slipped to make sure Anastasia was behaving; she rushed him and threw the sand into his face.

He grabbed at his eyes, bending over to brush away the antagonizing particles. A foot in his privates gave her payback for having let him near enough to leave a mark. Then a karate chop to his neck rendered him useless long enough for her to rush after Stasia, grab her hand and run to where the bike sat waiting by the street. Here there was traffic and people and witnesses. They couldn't be attacked here without drawing a lot of attention.

Sure enough, the two men who'd taken up the chase once again came only so close before they slowed to a quick walk in their direction, one calling for Stasia to come back. "Think hard before you do anything stupid, Stasia. We'll find you. Don't make any more trouble for you and your friend."

Ignoring their threats, Sophia rushed to the bike and started it. Stasia climbed on the seat behind, and they whirled away from the street. In no time, Sophia saw the headlights of the car their attackers had climbed into following them up the highway. On the left side, the brake light wasn't working. Good. Now she'd know for sure which car to watch out for.

Angry at her decision for wearing the one dress that would glow in the moonlight like a white truce-flag, she made herself as small as possible and gathered her skirts under her so as not to give them too much evidence they had the right motorcycle.

She purposely headed in the direction where she knew a lot of bikes traveled and wove between them easily, wanting to lose their pursuers.

Grinning, she next headed in the one direction a four-wheeled vehicle couldn't go. Off-road riding had been a favorite with her Yaya, and she'd taught Sophia all the better trails close to the city. Within ten minutes, watching for the broken light and seeing no vehicle like it, she again cruised the streets.

Making sure they'd lost the creeps, she headed in the direction where she knew there'd be hell to pay. It was time to return to the probable wrath of the man whose bike she'd borrowed without permission.

What bothered her... How the hell was she going to explain Stasia's appearance?

Chapter Fifteen

More anxious as the time crawled, Sam drank his first cup of coffee and then helped himself to a second. After serious debate, he'd decided not to react badly to Sophia's disappearing like she did. Hell, he understood her need for the time alone.

Using his phone, he'd read all the notes John-john had forwarded him about the agent and knew she'd biked a lot with her grandmother while living here during many summers. Her own mother had never enjoyed this mode of travel after an accident had hospitalized her as a teenager, so it had been her grandmother, Tanya, who'd taught Sophia how to ride a motorbike.

He knew this because she'd won a lot of contests in her teens, and when she'd received a prize ribbon for the first win, she'd attributed her ability to her grandmother, bragging about how her Yaya had won the same contest years earlier, and that she'd taught her everything she knew.

Rereading the ream of notes while waiting, he also learned about her shooting skills. Again, another of her many pastimes spent with Tanya Adamos while in Rhodes for summers.

He wished the older woman still lived because she must have been something in her youth. As a champion herself, she'd brought her granddaughter up to follow in her footsteps. No wonder the Bureau thought so highly of their agent that they'd trust her with this case.

Finally, he heard the sound he'd been waiting for over an hour to hear. She was pulling into the driveway. He stood to refill the coffee pot with water and brooded when his heartbeat sped up, and his mouth suddenly turned dry.

Play it cool, dude. Just let her do the talking.

***

Looking disheveled and much less spotless than when he'd seen her last, Sophia stepped into the kitchen first, followed by a very young, damp looking... huh?

A hooker!

She spoke first, saying the obvious. "You're still here."

"Ahhh... yes. You stole my transportation, remember? Who's your friend?"

Sophia quickly put her arm around the kid who'd backstepped as soon as she'd caught sight of Sam. Distancing herself from the stranger, the scared girl had to be coaxed to relax.

Sophia's manner turned convincing and gentle. "Don't worry, Stasia. He's a friend of mine. His name is Sam. He's cool."

"He's a cop." The girl didn't mince her words, her fear palpable.

Sophia looked stunned at the words, and she swung toward Sam who grinned and gave a negative shake of his head. "No, I'm not. Not now. But I used to be. I guess the label still shows." She watched as he purposely invaded the kid's space, held out his hand and waited until Stasia finally set hers there, gently sucking her into his web.

Handsome, sophisticated, and knowing his own power, he leaned down slightly so Stasia could see him clearly. Then he spoke, his voice mesmerizingly clear. "You're in trouble, honey. Look, I'll help any way I can. Don't worry now."

Sophia waited, her breath held, her pulse throbbing, all her feminine endings tingling, willing the kid to believe. When Stasia tiredly dropped her face onto their locked hands as if giving him power over her, the stress from the last rush of adrenaline oozed away, and Sophia felt a huge sense of relief.

They had a friend to help them. Thank God, because she needed to maintain a low profile while here in Rhodes working on her latest assignment. And absconding a trafficked teen hooker wasn't exactly what Sunny, her boss, would appreciate as her way of keeping things low-key.

Sam patted the girl's cheek and then stepped away. "I'm making coffee, and I found fresh bread and meat for sandwiches, so if you ladies would like to clean up, I'll get things ready. Then while you eat, you can tell me the trouble you're in, and I'll help in any way I can."

Pleased at his way of breaking up the awkward moment, Sophia urged Stasia to her grandmother's suite. The one empty room where she knew there would be clothes still hanging in the closet, clothes that her shrinking darling had worn during the last years of her life as she shriveled in size from the horrors of cancer.

Even then, her grandmother had refused to dress like a dowdy old woman, and so she'd bought stuff that even Sophia might find too youthful to choose. And, no doubt, would fit Stasia better than anything she herself could offer.

In moments, they entered the lovely pale green space. While Sophia scrounged in the drawers finding pajamas for Stasia, the dazed kid stood looking around as if she were in a palace.

Sophia left her to familiarize herself and used the combination to open the closet, coming back with a housecoat that would be perfect. "Here's some clothes you can change into, Stasia. The bathroom's through here. There's everything you need to wash and shampoo the sand from your hair. Come back into the kitchen when you're ready, okay?"

"Yes. I can do so. You're very kind, Sophia. I'm...
I'm..."

"You're going to cry if you keep talking. Just
relax, kiddo. You're safe here. We'll be waiting."

Once Stasia disappeared, Sophia stood in the
room she hadn't been able to enter earlier and felt
the presence of the woman who she'd loved so
dearly. The warmth she sensed let her know her
Yaya appreciated how Sophia had acted, and if
alive, would have done exactly the same thing.

She'd always worked with the underprivileged.
Spent hours at the church to help as many people
as possible. It would have tickled her to know
Sophia had rescued a helpless kitten from the
clutches of three cruel bulldogs. Smiling, Sophia
quickly went to her own room, took a cop's shower
every officer with a badge could do in under five
minutes, and was back in the kitchen dressed in
her jeans and T-shirt before Sam's sandwiches
were finished.

She stood in the doorway, watching the
powerful man move around with little hesitation.
Barney had promised to provide her with fresh
food to tide her over until she shopped, and the
smell of fresh-baked bread tantalized her taste
buds, causing her to realize she was hungry again.

She approached and knew from the way he'd
glanced sideways that he was totally aware she'd
been standing there.

"You're not mad that I took your motorcycle?"

"Nope. I could see you knew how to handle a bike. And you seemed to have sobered up enough to steal it. I decided to just wait it out and hope you'd behave."

Sophia's brow shot up, and she grinned in the same way that Bunny loved to tease her about... when he'd accuse her of being purposely bratty. "Behave?"

"Yeah, you know. Not get into any trouble. Take a short ride down memory lane and return looking the way you did when you left."

"I do look the same."

"I beg to differ. When you disappeared, your dress was clean, you still had one shoe, and there weren't any abrasions on your face. Wanna tell me what happened in the interim?"

Sophia heard the hardness that entered his tone when he mentioned the bruise. And she almost stepped back when his hand lifted and gently caressed the area on her cheek that still stung. Shocked, unable to move, she gazed back at his mesmerizing stare and answered.

"I went to the beach."

"Okay."

"I heard Stasia crying."

"She was alone?"

"Yes. I mean no. I mean she was alone when I first saw her. She was terrified."

"And you couldn't walk away." He didn't say it

like a question.

"No. I went to her and saw she'd been in the water and looked like a drowned kitten."

"Uh huh."

"Well what could I do?"

"Exactly."

"I had to help her. She was terrified."

"You already said that."

"Right. So, I brought her home."

"You forgot to mention the part where some asshole punched you. I want to know who so I can go back and nail the son of a bitch."

Sophia heard the menace. In fact, she felt it oozing around them and knew Sam meant every word. Why he would say such a thing, she had no idea. Yet he spoke with enough conviction that she realized he could and would if she gave him the information.

His confidence made her feel protected, and that's not something that any other man had made her feel ever before. Not knowing how to handle so much emotion, she forced herself to turn away from his piercing brown scrutiny that could steal her breath away.

Everything would have been fine if he'd let her go. But he didn't. Instead, he used his hands to turn her back toward him, lowered his mouth, and then kissed her. Not a soft kiss one might give as a first try, no not soft at all.

But it wasn't a hard, hurting force of his mouth

on hers either. He just lowered his lips until they hovered inches above hers. Until she could smell the warmth of his coffee breath and feel the heat of his thrilling presence. Then he searched her eyes.

With anyone else trying a stunt like this, she'd have had them either on the floor writhing from being kicked in a place to take their mind off sex. Or, she'd have maneuvered herself away from their manipulation and made them understand her lack of interest.

Instead, with Sam, she sighed, returned his sultry gaze, and waited until his lips were taking possession of hers. Everything about the subsequent kiss blew her mind. The taste of him, the softness inside his mouth when he opened to her tongue and gave her his. The groan of relief she heard as if he'd been waiting forever for this moment.

What the hell was she thinking? How in the world had he gotten under her shield? He needed to leave. She had a job to do. Pulling away from his warmth, she wiped at her mouth as if his kiss needed to be removed and turned her back.

"Goodness, that's enough of that nonsense. I need to look after Stasia, and you need to leave."

"No. You need to tell me the truth about what went down at the beach tonight. And I need to check it out. There's no way a kid her age should be running away, trying to drown herself. She's terrified and looks like she has good reason to be.

Just the fact that she had a man coming after her, putting you in a position where you had to fight him off, tells me there's much more to the story."

They didn't hear Stasia's return.

"There were three men. And Sophia won."

Chapter Sixteen

Sophia couldn't believe Stasia would be so open at the very time when she'd much prefer her to remain secretive. Yet Sam had a way about him... of gaining trust.

He stepped in before Sophia could speak. "Come and have a sandwich, Stasia. Then you can tell us about your trouble, and we'll help you stay safe."

Stasia came forward slowly, looking first at Sophia as if she sensed her displeasure. No doubt, the kid had perfected her sensitivity for any kind of tension, and she'd picked up on Sophia's disgruntled emotions.

She stepped close and whispered, "Should I not speak with him, Sophia?" Stasia waited for her answer and would no doubt have done exactly what Sophia wanted.

But she couldn't refuse this kid his protection.

Though the very last thing she wanted right now was to have this discerning, sharp-eyed sex toy anywhere near her, how could she refuse for Stasia to get help in any way possible? "It's fine. Tell us both why you were trying to get away from the men who came to force you back to the hotel."

At this point, Sam stopped her and headed to the small table where they could all relax. "You're shaking, Stasia. And there's no need for you to be frightened any longer. You'll be able to think better after you have something in your belly. Eat, and we'll pick up the story after you're done." He placed her plate with the sandwich down in front of her and added a cup of the steaming hot coffee.

Sophia fetched the sugar and cream and added a dish of her favorite apple pastries, a sweet treat from Barney that she'd noticed wrapped in the brown, grease-soaked bakery bag on the counter. Then she took her place.

Once they'd all taken a first bite, Sam kept them amused with his first observations of Rhodes and how he'd taken to the historical location. "I guess one of my first shocks was seeing shops where they had fish tanks for people to submerge their feet so the fish could eat all the old skin. Never saw that before."

Sophia laughed. "It's rejuvenating. The tanks are cleaned every day and the fish are well fed each morning. Some people think the owners starve the fish so they will clean the feet, but it's not so. It's just what they do."

"Not with my feet they won't."

"Big baby. You really can't be afraid of tiny little fish."

"I can if I'm ticklish and would react like a giggling idiot if anything gets near my toes."

Sophia caught on to his joking manner and teased him more. "Then I guess snorkeling in the incredible bays around here is out of the question. There's millions of fish there."

"Oh, no you don't. We both know the difference. Those fish don't dine off your body."

Sophia had to laugh at his expression. "Okay, you got me there."

They finished their sandwiches and Sophia could see that it had helped calm Stasia enough that she'd reached for another of the delicious apple fritters.

Finally, Sam started the serious discussion. "Start at the beginning, Stasia. Where you're from and why you're in Greece."

"My name is Anastasia Dedov. I was born in St. Petersburg, but when my mother died last year, my father brought all his children to Sochi. There are seven of us. I'm the oldest girl."

"Were you in school there?" Sophia wanted to get an overall picture of this girl's existence before she was brought to Greece.

Settling into her story, Stasia sat on her hands and leaned forward, her expression grim. "No. My father can't afford school for us all. I work at garment factory. One day, two men come to factory and promise us better life. A future in Europe where we earn good wages and live happy life. We believe them. My father use his small savings to help me pay fare so I can come."

Sophia couldn't imagine a caring father allowing a young girl to go off with strangers. "Did he meet those men?"

"No. They didn't give any time. We have to follow orders, have money with us and be ready to leave next day."

Sam asked, "And you believed them?"

"Yes. Until we arrive at ship. It was horrible. Trapped in a box for many days. Lucky, we were small group, only fifteen of us. We had little food, a small toilet with curtain that become a... an ugly mess, and foam mats to sleep on. There were more girls, and so we were safe from boys even though they tried to corner us and act like... like dogs."

Sophia couldn't begin to comprehend the nightmare trip, yet she knew this kind of unimaginable horror happened in many places in the world.

"Some of girls from same factory didn't make it. Two died on way over. Stella lost her mind and kill herself. And Alice become sick. We find her dead three days before we arrive. It was worst thing, not being able to bury them. We had to use plastic curtain for bodies and to stop smells. God help me for hating these... those poor girls by the time they let us loose."

Wanting to turn her away from the mental pictures and painful memories that showed so completely on her small face, Sophia said, "You speak English very well. Were you taught it as a child?"

"Oh no, while we recovered from trip, they make us learn English emersion classes. They beat us if we don't learn to speak quickly. They don't let us sleep more than a few hours each night. The rest of the time, we take lessons. Even now, after they put us to work, we must take lessons when not with customer."

Sophia knew the answer, but she had to make sure. "What exactly is it you're made to do?"

As if it was the most obvious and acceptable answer, Stasia began. "Service clients in any way they want. I'm one of luckier girls. Others have to accept beatings and worse disgusting demands from... from sick people. They haven't treated me so harsh. But tonight, my friend Mona is unwell, and they want I should service the pig who always picks her. She's an animal who hits and bites, smokes cigarettes to burn. I couldn't. I run away. I'd rather die than be in same room with crazy woman."

Sophia revealed her shock before she could stop herself. "A woman?"

"Yes. There are many women who like to be with

us. Some are nice, bring presents – earrings and makeup. And they treat us good. Others are worse than men who just have their... their way and leave."

Sam cut in, "Are these so-called customers Greeks who live here in Rhodes or mainly the tourists?"

"Both. Greeks are more careful. Same ones come often. But tourists know they only be here for little time. They act like... like they can behave any way they want."

"Where do these men keep you when you're not brought to the hotels?"

"We go to bars and parties too."

"But where do you sleep?"

"I don't know. I mean, I know house is not too big where they keep us in basement, and it is surrounded by weeds and dry grass, like farmland. There are hundreds of olive trees around, that I know. But where it is from city, they never let us see. We travel always in back of van with no windows, and they put curtain at front so we can't see."

"Do customers come there?" Sophia wanted to get a good idea of the arrangement so when she reported this to the local authorities; she could give them more details.

"Net... I mean no. There is a fancy place where we spend much time waiting for customers to come. Tonight, it was special at this hotel, because crazy bitch had party where she wants ten of us to come. It is why I can run. They can't keep us all together, and I find way to es-escape."

"You were very lucky." Sam had no doubt that the only reason Stasia had the guts to run was because her previous background of loving care had given her acute motivation that produced an innate cunning many others would never achieve. Fourteen or forty, this ingenuity couldn't be taught. He'd seen it in his own line of work. The best-trained soldiers could never compete with someone born with the skills of a natural-born fighter.

"Yes, lucky that Sophia find me. If not, they make me go back, and they will beat me and hurt me after they give me to crazy lady. It is why I want to kill myself. I keep swimming. I want to die. But I can't stop saving myself. I'm no good for nothing. I can't do anything right."

When the tears came, they gushed from her all at once. The girl in her grandmother's pretty pajamas with pink kisses all over the pants and the fuzzy housecoat to match made her look like any regular teenager back home. But the words that had poured from her mouth created such a horrifying picture that Sophia sat stunned.

Not Sam. He moved in and wrapped his big arms around the girl to hug her close. When she struggled, his husky voice calmed her. "No, don't fret, honey. I'm not here to upset you. I would never hurt you, ever. And no one else will ever get at you again because they'd have to come through me first, and that will never happen. You're safe now, little girl. Sophia and I will help you."

"But, my passport. They have it. And my money, they have. Me, I have nothing." Her voice broke up as she struggled with her English.

Sophia knelt in front of Stasia and held her hands. "You have us, Stasia. Sam is right. You're not alone any longer."

While Stasia used the back of her hand to clean the drips from her nose, Sophia used a tissue to wipe at the cascading tears. She'd never felt so sorry for anyone before or so ashamed of the world she lived in that could wrong a precious human being so badly.

Chapter Seventeen

Sam felt like a vicious out-of-control bronco was kicking him in the stomach. The pain swamped him, and he had no way to shut off the tap. To do so would mean stopping Stasia from telling her story. And that couldn't happen. She needed to talk, and they needed to listen.

And listen they did. She talked for an hour, about her poor heartbroken father who missed his wife and about the other children who she loved dearly and had wanted to help by earning good wages to share with them.

About the monsters who'd tricked her and taken such advantage. And the life she now lived, full of fear and self-hatred. The fighting amongst the others in the house where wretchedness filled the days and their only escape meant a few hours of sleeping forgetfulness.

In his profession, he was well aware of the

modern form of slavery going on in so many places around the globe. Undocumented migrants whose immigration status was exploited for profit across a wide variety of industries. These unfortunate people were being used and abused by those who didn't give a good God-damn about anything or anybody. Money was their motive, their idol, and turning a blind eye their way of dealing with the human misery.

Some might say the luckier victims were used as slaves to do menial labor, including debt bondage, when a person is forced to work for free to pay off a debt. Also, child slavery, forced marriage, domestic servitude where innocents are made to work through violence and intimidation

Like anyone with a heart, everything about these operations made him want to throw the sick shitheads involved in a cell and let them rot. Maybe it was time for him to get personally involved, him and his people.

Yet he was hamstrung by the promise he'd made his sister. He couldn't rock this particular boat until his niece and nephew were safely back home where they belonged.

Chapter Eighteen

Shocked to see Sam waiting to talk after leading Stasia to her room and settling her there, Sophia stepped into the kitchen and stood by the door. She had no intention of getting anywhere near the guy.

Right now, her feelings were so fragile, she'd be an easy mark for the experienced womanizer. Having a man's arms hold and comfort her would be a godsend right about now, but no way was it going to happen.

She'd already loosened her restrictions once tonight and blamed it on the residual alcohol. This time she'd have no excuse but tiredness, a sad heart, and the unsettling vibes tingling between them.

He waited for her to speak, and she did the same. Silence stretched and the tension built. If she had to describe the ridiculous sensations, she'd compare them to live wires simultaneously nudging at each other, igniting sparks. It was ridiculous, and she wasn't having it. Not now for crissakes. She didn't have time for any of this nonsense.

"You need to leave."

"No, we need to talk."

"Truthfully, I've had about as much talking tonight as I can take. Go."

"I promised Stasia to be here for her. I meant it." The stubborn expression on his handsome face let her know he was serious.

"She's safe with me." Sophia wished she could pull out her FBI shield as proof.

"For now."

"For as long as it takes to get her help."

"What do you plan to do?"

"I have connections in Rhodes. My grandmother knew many people in high places. I can go to her old friend the mayor."

"Can you trust him?"

"Yes, of course, or I wouldn't think of taking Stasia to see him."

"You're planning on taking her around the city? It's dangerous."

"We'll be careful. Look, I can't talk about this right now. Whatever you want to say will have to wait. She'll be fine. I'll be with her."

"Oh, I see. So, will you also be bringing her along on the family barbecue?"

Son of a bitch! She couldn't take that chance. Manos would be there, and she had a feeling this group of immigrants brought to Greece could be his doing. Didn't Bruner tell her that they had confirmation that Manos Savas was implicated in this whole black market scheme? *Fuck me...* she couldn't leave Stasia alone until she knew she was safe. And this island was a small place. People talked. Descriptions of a young girl she suddenly took in could bring results.

"Fine, come and check up on us if you wish. But leave now." She saw the stubborn refusal on his face and added a beseeching request. "Please."

It worked. His expression softened, and his grin gave her the answer she desperately needed. "Okay, sugar. But... I'll be here tomorrow."

Chapter Nineteen

Sam mounted his bike and left Sophia's home. Unable to uncharge his over-flowing batteries, he headed to where he could find release. After listening to Stasia describe her situation, his need to kick ass had ramped up, and from history, he knew he'd never get to sleep.

He drove around the city and headed to one of the beach areas, wondering if it was the same one where Sophia had met up with Stasia. Sure, there's the hotel she mentioned. He slowed and drove by while checking out the area where he figured the girls had found each other.

He didn't pay attention to the vehicle behind him pulling up closer until he noticed that the left brake light didn't work. Good. He pulled over and figured they'd do so too. Then he leaned on the bike seat and waited to see what the two dudes had planned.

Both men were large and wore the typical island styles but all in black. They sported bald heads and mean features and could have been twins, they looked so much alike. Oh, not in their features as much as in their manners, but both were about the same large size and one had an eye affliction if the red bloodshot appearance was anything to go by.

They didn't disappoint. He knew the chances were they'd have made a note of the license number on the bike and guessed they had some questions they intended asking.

God help them, he had a few answers he was dying to give them too. He wasn't kept waiting for long.

"That your bike?"

"It's a rental."

"You the only driver?"

"None of your business."

There was a hesitating glance between the twins before the red-eyed fellow finally spoke, "You need to come with us."

"Why?"

"We want to talk with you."

Realizing he couldn't take the chance that Manos might be one of the talkers, he chuckled and answered, sarcastic as hell, "I have no intention of going anywhere with you."

If he wasn't having so much fun poking the tiger, he'd have noticed the third man approaching from behind. As it was, he swung around just in time for his cheek to connect with the fist coming his way.

Lights went off in his brain, and eighty-six million sneaky neurons woke up from their peaceful existence. They warned him in no uncertain terms, he didn't like pain.

Nor did he let it slow him down. At the same time as he grabbed at the punishing fist still there, he kicked the closest dude in his jewels and the resulting scream gave him a wonderfully satisfying feeling. Then he swung the sneak-attacker over his shoulder to land on the second twin. Watching them wrestling to get to their feet and come at him again, he waited until they had untangled and kicked the second twin in the head knowing he wouldn't revive soon. Then he went in for the face-puncher.

Bastard had caught him out and needed a lesson. They grappled, and he took another hit to his stomach but had the satisfaction of grabbing the guy's head and forcing it to meet his upcoming knee. The resultant crunch of nose cartilage made his day. Now he could go back to his room and catch up on his sleep.

He got on his bike and headed to the dealership near his hotel and left the bike in their parking lot. Best to dump this baby now.

He'd clear out of his room first thing in the morning and find another. Best not tease the dragon any further now that he'd woken it up.

Chapter
Twenty

Sophia made a phone call the next morning to set up an appointment with the mayor and was pleasantly surprised when she was given a time later that day. The mayor had an unexpected cancellation that she could fill if she wished.

Good. The sooner she met up with one of her favorites of Yaya's friends the better. Old Hamilton Alexopoulos had been around since she could remember, and the wonderful old man had always treated her like a princess.

Sophia trusted him more than many other people she knew and felt sure Stasia's problems were going to be solved very soon. This wasn't only about saving her new friend. Others confined where she'd been imprisoned needed help as well.

After the girls had their breakfast, and Stasia offered to clean up, Sophia went to her grandmother's closet to find a younger-looking, less sophisticated-styled outfit for Stasia. The moment she stepped inside, her Yaya's favorite scent surrounded her. Memories flooded and tears followed.

Angry at her loss of composure, Sophia swallowed and searched the racks for something a young girl would look appropriate wearing. As she flung the hangers past her, one particular outfit appeared, and she burrowed her face in the silky red material.

The dress her grandmother wore to the last ball they attended wrinkled in her clutching hands. Loss overcame her so suddenly that she sank to the floor, weeping.

Her Yaya had looked fragile as a flower wearing the gown, desperately trying to hide her frailty. The garment hadn't worked. All that night, Sophia had stayed close, fearing something was wrong, yet not knowing what it was.

Fucking cancer. Took the best and left the rest to mourn.

Stasia called out from the hallway, "Sophia, can I help you with anything?"

Straightening, forcing herself to her feet, Sophia smoothed the now crinkled material and rehung the garment on the hanger. Then she reached for a very plain blue A-line outfit she'd never seen before. "Come try this one, Stasia. It's short enough and should fit you quite well."

As soon as Stasia saw the dress, her face lit up,

and she reached for the hanger. "I had dress very... ahh, samular... I mean, similar, but they took away. All they want for us to wear are ugly, bad clothes to make us look like whores."

Sophia stepped close to Stasia and held her arms firmly so she couldn't turn away. "Listen to me! You are not a whore. That title belongs to a person who's purposely made the choice to live that life... you didn't. There's a huge difference. You're a victim, Stasia. You hear me?"

Stasia's lip trembled, and she nodded. Then she shyly lifted her hand to point at the tears still visible on Sophia's face. "I'm sorry about your babushka. The old people are precious, I know. Mine lived with us years before she died. We missed her a long time."

"Thank you, Stasia. My grandmother was special. So you know, she made this closet into a safe retreat in case of any crisis. The door has a combination lock from both sides. You must remember the four numbers one, one, four, seven should you ever need a safe place in this house."

"One, one, four, seven. I remember."

"Good. Yaya had been alone when an intruder broke in a few years ago. She never wanted to feel at the mercy of anyone again. She hid in here but knew if he looked, he could get at her. Now no one can. She had a phone installed in that slot there – see where her hats are, just below. It's always left there in case of any emergency."

A smile broke out over the young girl's features, the first real smile Sophia had seen so far. "Your baba was smart lady."

"Very smart. You'd have liked her, and she'd have loved you. Young people were her favorite persons to hang with. One day, I'll tell you more about her but now we need to get ready. We don't want to keep the old mayor waiting. Besides, the fact is, I can't wait to see him again. He's a pet. You'll like him."

***

"What do you mean Hamilton Alexopoulos isn't here? The man hasn't missed a day in years."

"Look, he's gone, like in dead."

"He passed away?" Sophia stood in front of the new secretary, a tall, skinny dude with attitude, and her shock kept her arguing. "But I talked to him on the phone just a few months ago." He'd called to commiserate with her about Tanya's death yet again. And how much he missed his darling friend. Oh, they knew she was sick, had been for years, but no one expected her to develop pneumonia and be gone within hours.

Sophia had been pulled off her assignment so she could fly back for the funeral. Her and her father had suffered through the formalities, and when the lawyers read the will and Sophia had been named her beneficiary, no one had been surprised.

During those terrible days of grief, Hamilton

and her father had been her lifesavers, not letting her stay alone, being there for her so she could get through the saddest time since her mother died. And Barney had made all the arrangements to save her from having to deal with obstacles and fine print that she was in no condition to handle.

How did she not know the old man was gone? She'd be discussing this with Barney first chance. Right now, she needed to keep her cool so she could meet with the new mayor.

The haughty employee waited for her to settle down while Stasia stood by her side still wearing her borrowed sunglasses, glancing around the grand room. Prominent photographs displayed on the wall of earlier mayors stood out and suddenly Stasia froze. She pointed to the one hanging next to an older man and asked, "Is he mayor now?"

Barely giving her any attention, the snotty jerk answered, "Yes. That's Mayor Paolo Diakos. He can see you now. This way, if you please."

Abruptly, Stasia became sickly looking and gripped her stomach. "I'm not good, Sophia. Please, I must use ladies' room."

"Miss, the mayor is a busy man. He cannot wait for you. If you don't go in now, it'll be weeks before I can make you a new appointment."

For the first time, Sophia saw the idiot rattled and could give a shit. "Look, my friend isn't well. Don't worry about another appointment. We were here to see Hamilton anyway." She saw Stasia speeding to a doorway with the restroom sign high on the wall above. Then she turned to the disgusted-looking fellow reaching for the intercom phone. She stopped him.

"What happened to Mayor Alexopoulos. How did he die?"

"I really don't know for sure, Miss Dunne. They found him still in his car at the bottom of the cliff off Atki Kanari. Maybe the old man had a heart attack or too much to drink. Who knows?"

And you could care less Sophia thought as soon as the words left his mouth. She did not like this guy and couldn't leave his space fast enough. But she also wouldn't go without setting him straight. "Listen here, that old man was a saint. He helped the people in this city, and they loved him. Let's hope the new mayor can carry on his legacy."

She stomped away before she set this sneering bastard on his ass and went to find Stasia. When she opened the door, she saw a distraught girl shaken and white-faced. Sophia found it hard to believe she was the same calm person who'd walked in with her just a few minutes earlier.

"Stasia! What's happened?"

"He is customer?"

Confused, Sophia asked, "The secretary?"

"No, not him. The mayor. I recognize him from picture. He likes more than one girl at a time. He is a pig."

Gentle Jesus! "You're sure?"

"Yes. Yes. He must not see me. He is friend with Manos."

Suddenly, her ears perked up, and Sophia got serious. "This Manos, who is he? You never mentioned him last night."

"He is big boss. Everyone is scared of him. The woman at the house is his person – he depends on her most. She is in charge of girls. Remember, I told you last night about Fedrika? Well, she is bitch who keeps girls in line."

"How old is this female? Is she Greek?"

"I don't know. Her hair is light, but could be dyed, and she's wrinkled like elephant. She's old, at least forty, and smokes many packages of cigarettes a day, and... and she drinks much vodka in big glass. I hate her."

Chapter
Twenty-one

Taking care to get Stasia back to Tanya's car unseen, Sophia drove her to the house and wasn't surprised to find Sam waiting for them, leaning against a different but gorgeous dark green bike.

He watched them approach before he unclasped his arms and straightened to stand upright. The way he moved, unhurried with a laziness like a wild lion about to survey his kingdom, made her pulse quicken. This man was a menace to her equilibrium, and he needed to leave.

Then she closed in and saw the bruise on his face and a whole different feeling took over. Angry, but not at him, she stalked closer and asked, "Who were you brawling with?"

"Just a couple of guys looking for trouble. It's no biggie."

"Oh, I get it. You started a fight for shits and giggles."

"Who said I started it?"

Sophia didn't know what would satisfy her temper more. To slap the teasing grin off his face or have him leave and not come back. "What do you want?"

Stasia approached, almost skipping towards the jerk, obviously happy to see him. "Hi Sam. Have you come to see us?"

The silent glare happening between Sophia and Sam finally registered, and the young girl looked scared. "I'm sorry. Are you angry? Did I say something wrong?"

Taking pity on the youngster, Sophia stopped scowling at the man, and instead put her arm around Stasia and led her to the house. "Of course not. Sam is coming in for a quick cup of coffee." A thought crossed her mind and she added, "And he can stay to keep you company while I go to see an old friend."

***

Sam was stubborn, she'd give him that much, but she wouldn't be deterred. "Look, I need to visit Yanis and find out what really happened to Mayor Alexopoulos. Stasia told you about the man who's now mayor. Well the old mayor was a dear friend of both me and Tanya. I can't believe he'd drive off a road he's driven on all his life. I need to check into what could have happened to him."

"Yet if you go out in public, those men might have spies out watching for you. They could get to you."

She held her hand out and said, "Give me your phone." When he did so, she added her particulars and then gave him her phone to do the same. "Okay, we're connected. You can keep tabs on me. You have my GPS. Stay here with Stasia. She can't come with me. I won't take that chance."

"Goddammit, woman, but you're stubborn. She'll be safe here alone. It's you I'm worried about. I need to go with you."

"No. I'll be fine. As my Dad always says, 'stay where you're to 'til I comes where you're at.'" She grinned at his perplexed stare. "Nevermind. Look, I know my way around Old Town. I can hide where no one could find me. If I get into trouble, I'll text you." Unwilling to carry on arguing, she walked to the door and left the house. The next sound coming from the yard was his bike starting up.

"Blasted hell. Damn woman stole my bike again."

Chapter
Twenty-two

Sophia hadn't taken time to change and was still wearing the dressy summer outfit of light blue pants and flowing top she'd chosen for her visit with Hamilton. Not willing to let Sam badger her any longer, she'd grabbed her small over-the-shoulder purse that held her gear, including a small revolver she always carried and headed the bike toward the old town.

She had no regrets using Sam's transportation again. He shouldn't leave the key in the ignition if he didn't want it taken. Her own Harley was stored in the garage, and she hadn't had the time to bring it out and clean it up. It was one of her chores she'd decided on doing later that day. For now, this monster would work just fine.

Easing her way into the market area, she took the most convenient route to where her friend Yanis worked at his fish spa near the main plaza. Not wanting to take the bike through the narrower lanes where his business was located, she parked near the quay and entered the Eleftherias gate, then wandered the streets to find her destination.

There were hordes of people milling around, everyone shopping for just that perfect souvenir. As she neared her objective – a small place nestled in between a shop that sold wonderful Greek linens on one side, and a jewelry store on the other – she saw Yanis sitting in the sunshine, visiting with some of the tourists.

Most were eager for information and leery about actually putting any part of their body in the fish tanks. It made Sophia happy that no one was taking advantage of the spa. That meant she wouldn't have to share her friend.

As she approached the middle-aged man in the blue shirt and white shorts, he rose and walked toward her, a smile lighting his handsome face, his hands reaching. "Sophia, ómorfo korítsi. Darling girl. You look beautiful as always." He hugged her, kissed both her cheeks, and then stepped back while he held her hands out and forced her to stand still under his inspection.

"You're glowing. It's a man. You're attracted but unwilling to admit it. Who is he?"

"Yanis, stop your gypsy-like sorcery and quit teasing. I can see how much fun you're having." His deep blue eyes were twinkling with merriment, and she loved the ambiance he always revealed when she was with him. She gave a yank to his long white ponytail teasingly and added, "I'm here to say hello and catch up with the local news."

"And to get a treatment."

"Of course. I'll feed the little piranhas in your tanks, and like when I was a little girl, it will bring other customers."

"You were my best draw for the leery tourists. Once they saw a small girl giggling from the tickles, it made them less worried."

"Those were such fun days, Yanis. Mom and Yaya would go off for lunch, and I'd beg them to leave me with you."

"I begged them too." He laughed with her and waited for her to settle on the high bench above the large fish tanks full of tiny Garra rufa. As she started to show first the heel of her foot for the doctor fish to begin their work, he took the other foot in his hand, and using a special pumice he'd had soaking in disinfectant, he began scrubbing at the bottoms.

His searching Mediterranean blue eyes studied her closely, and he became serious. "What's wrong my darling? Tell Yanis."

"I went to see Hamilton, and a new secretary, not the same man he's had with him for years, told me that he'd passed."

Anger colored Yanis's face, and he stopped his chore to glare at her. "It's a terrible shame. The papers said he died from overindulgence. He drove off the—"

Interrupting him, Sophia exclaimed. "I know, but that's not possible. I've never known Hamilton to drink more than a few sips of wine. No way he'd be too drunk to drive."

"My exact thoughts. I went to the funeral, and his daughters were too distraught to make much sense. It happened so suddenly no one had been prepared. When they finally questioned the verdict, the new mayor said his blood-alcohol level read over the limit. To protect the old man's name, his office told the papers he'd had a heart attack."

"Did you talk to the emergency room doctor, the one who looked after him when they brought him in?"

"Sophia, they took him straight to the morgue." Yanis patted her leg comfortingly and added, "He wouldn't have wanted anyone to see him all broken. He cared about his family too much."

"Do you believe he killed himself because he was drunk?"

"Not for a moment. I went to the police, and the new Commander, a man I never met before, tried to appear like he cared about my suspicions. But I know better. It didn't concern him at all. I took a dislike to that man."

Using the Greek name for the city, she spoke. "Something disturbing is happening in Rodos, Yanis." She let the tiny sensations from the fish sooth as she explained what occurred the night before. She told him about Stasia and how they'd met. When she'd finished, his expression darkened, and he made a statement with a firmness she didn't question. She'd never doubted his strange powers, and this prediction gave her chills.

"My lovely, you must be careful not to awaken the beast. His cruelty knows no bounds. The new mayor and his associates will do anything to protect that which he's built. It's about the money, Sophia, mia. It's about the vast amounts of money."

"Isn't it always? Some people will do anything for wealth and power. I need to find a way to help Stasia and her friends."

"If you give me a few days, I will gather together some of the older citizens on council, and we will find a way to overcome this problem."

"Don't let the new mayor find out what you're up to. Stasia swears he's one of their best customers."

"Disgusting pig."

"Funny you should say that. It's exactly what she calls him."

"I know."

Chapter Twenty-thre e

Sam and Stasia played a game of cards while they waited for Sophia to return.

"Where did you learn to play Rummy, Stasia?"

"It's what we do at our place. You know, pass time when not study English."

"I see. How many are there living with you?"

"It changes. They always move us from one place to another."

"Approximately."

"Maybe fifteen, maybe twenty. Sometimes there are less. I think lucky ones are bonded to families who make orders for... helpers."

"Helpers?"

"Yes, like nanny for children, or nurse for old person. They take... ahh, not so pretty girls for these places. Even boys can be bonded. Of course, they keep some to work in rooms. Sam, for first time in my life I wish to be born with pimples and ugly eyes."

Sam stared at her and added a droll tone to his voice on purpose. He dragged out the one word teasingly, "Real-ly?"

Looking guilty but steadfast, she growled, "Yes. Yes. Before I come to these men, I like being my father's pretty girl. Now, I'm sorry to look in mirror. I'd rather be ugly as dog – like what they called Alicia. Ugly as dog doesn't seem so bad when I hear she is safe in a home with children to care for."

"And earning a pittance for all the hard work they no doubt are forcing her to do. She'll be tied to those people for years as she pays off her debt, and Stasia, there'll be no extra money for her to send home, not unless she goes without the bare necessities herself. Oh, some lucky ones will end up with families who will treat them kindly, but the majority are in for many years of forced labor and confinement."

"Still... Sam, I would wish to be one of those. What they make me do is like... like animals." As she talked, her hand reached for the black mole on her left cheek, a place her hand often searched when she was agitated. "Now that I'm free, I will never let another person touch my person again."

From the look of conviction on her young face and the glare of loathing in her eyes, Sam had no doubt of her sincerity. "Honey, one day someone will come along and teach you how real love feels. Then you'll be able to let go of this nightmare."

"I don't deserve a good person to love me. I am unclean." She said it with such conviction, Sam thought carefully about his response before arguing.

"Okay, granted Stasia, you're not perfect. None of us are. But what's important is you care. About yourself, and your family and all that love you have inside will eventually find a mate to whom your heart matters more than your past." Sam reached up slowly so as not to startle her, and he gently rubbed the black spot where her own hand had nervously traveled. He smiled at her and added, "trust me, one day you will be able to put this terrible experience behind you and move on."

"Sam, I just want to go home. To my papa and my brothers and sisters."

"I know, honey. And you will. Soon. I promise." Sam heard the bike drive into the garden, and he went to the window to make sure it was Sophia.

When she stepped into the room, she must have sensed the emotions emanating from the youngster. Ignoring him, she hurried to the young girl who sat with her arms wrapped tightly over her head while her face remained hidden against her raised knees. "Don't worry, Stasia. Just as soon as we can get everyone working together, cleaning up the corruption that seems to be happening on the island, you will be free. I've spoken to my friend Yanis, who years earlier was a professor at the University, and he knows the politics on Rodos. He's lived here for many years and is closely involved with the powerful people. He's going to help us."

Sam listened to Sophia's reassuring words, but he also examined her expression and knew in an instant that something was terribly wrong.

Chapter
Twenty-four

By the time they were alone in the kitchen on the pretense of making lunch, Sophia sensed that Sam's frustration levels had risen to where he had a hard time being cool. His first question proved her right.

"What's going on?"

"Chill, boy-o. My friend Yanis is going to get us some answers to the questions about old Mayor Alexopoulos. He doesn't believe the man drove off the cliff because of overindulgence either. He sensed something was wrong at the time and asked questions about his death, but the *new* police commander put him off with bullshit." She purposely emphasized the one word to draw his attention.

He stiffened. "They have a new person in charge of the police. In other words, they've managed to infiltrate the areas in the government where detection for their underhanded activities will likely go unnoticed."

"Bingo!" She watched his face.

"What do you know about this guy?"

"Not a lot. Seems he arrived from Athens and was given the job by the slimy, devious, Mayor Diakos. They're old friends according to Yanis."

Sam leaned back against the table, hands on either side gripping the rim. He crossed his legs, his posture that of a man used to being in charge. He looked the embodiment of military. Hell, even Stasia had questioned his status. To her, it screamed cop. Caught out, he'd admitted to a past in the occupation, but she never did learn what he did today. She watched him closely, his expression, and the way he handled himself.

Who was this guy?

"Convenient, don't you think?" His words got through her mind-shift.

"Excuse me?"

He reached for his coffee mug still steaming and sipped as he watched her over the rim. "I was referring to the guy now in charge of law enforcement on the island." Realizing her mind had wandered, sarcasm appeared as he muttered. "Wh-at?"

"Question."

"Okay."

Though his cocky attitude still had her flummoxed, she'd swear he was in criminal investigative work. He knew how to intimidate, and he interrogated in the same way any ranking officer might do with total expectations of an answer.

"What did you say you do in the real world, Sam?"

***

Sam hadn't anticipated this question and was glad he'd practiced a reply when it came.

"I'm with the Air Force, home after three missions overseas."

"What do you do for them?"

"I'm a mechanic."

"Bullshit."

"Pardon me?"

"You heard me. You're lying, you're no mechanic." She knew it.

"I used to be."

"Not now. And quit being contrary."

"I've done a lot of things in my life—"

"Get to the point, Sam. What line of work are you in *now*?"

He hesitated. Somehow it seemed important he didn't lie to this girl. She wouldn't be one to easily forgive, and the way he was beginning to feel about her, he couldn't take the chance of earning her anger, or worse, her mistrust.

"I own a private, high-classed security firm which is mainly situated overseas in various locations, though I'm thinking to expand the firm in the Washington area soon. We offer stability and protection to people and locations experiencing turmoil. Our men and women are often called on to work with global commercial customers, numerous law enforcement and intelligence organizations, and even allied governments worldwide. Our services include armed personal escorts, executive protection and support, crowd control, and maritime security."

Holy shit! Was this for real?

"Why are you here? In Rhodes?"

"I told you. I'm on vacation. My sister, Sissy, recommended this place." The minute the name left his mouth, he knew she had him.

Sissy! Suddenly she looked awed. "You head the Reagan Group. That's why you looked familiar."

Sam's interest spiked. She knew about his company. That added another star on her growing list of gold. This chick's potential blossomed every time he was in her company. His hands itched to reach and touch, and as if he were just an interested guy on vacation looking for romantic entertainment, he fantasized about taking her to his bed and making her moan with delight.

Only he had to clear that sweet picture from his mind and concentrate on why he was really in Rhodes in the first place. His sister needed him, and now, so did Stasia. He couldn't afford to step into Sophia's space and cover her mouth with his while his hands traveled her hot bod.

No way.

Not a good idea,

Then why the hell he did just that surprised the bejesus out of him.

Another question he ignored but made him curious as hell, was why she let him. She just stood there while he scooped her face into his hands so he could hold her in place while he tested her lips and the softness of the skin on her face and neck.

She even arched her head slightly to give him better access. Her lips were soft and drew him in. Her taste beguiled him into losing his sanity. Her sweetness could be his downfall. Oh God, he shouldn't...

***

When his warm hands worked their way up her arms, caressing them and making her skin scream with joy, she relaxed into the rapture. She hadn't felt this way before – ever. With any man. In her whole life. Never.

Swelling sensations devastated all her sensibilities. If she didn't stop his hands from finding her aching breasts soon, she'd be leading him to her room and having her way with him.

His moan stayed her hands from pushing him away from her. Instead, they crawled around his neck and hugged him closer. Giving him access to her body so he could touch at will. Her back, her waist and finally grasp and squeeze her bottom. God, the next step was complete surrender.

***

Just as he was beginning to believe he had her fully primed, she whispered in an incredibly stressed voice, "If you don't behave and back off right now you cheeky bastard, I'll have to tell your sister, the Governor, you're trying to seduce her agent instead of doing your job."

Son of a bitch! So close...

Chapter
Twenty-five

Sophia's shock had kept her quiet. While Sam moved in on her, she'd been working it out in her mind that he must be Governor Regan's brother. And the only reason he'd come on to her at the restaurant in the first place was to infiltrate her mission to remove his niece and nephew from his brother-in-law.

It made total sense. Why he'd latched on to her, and why he was doing so now. His sister must have put him up to it. He didn't want to take any chances that she'd ignore him, and he'd be out of the picture. Did he even know she was FBI?

Fury engaged. She zeroed back to what his lips were doing. She shouldn't have – it proved to be her downfall. This man knew his way around a woman's body... and her emotions.

Carried away and fighting to keep her cool, she decided to give him just a few more minutes of foreplay before she lowered the boom. Except, she had to admit that everything he was doing to her, turned her on more.

His hands worked magic and his lips tasted better than any others. His sighs of enjoyment soon turned to pants of anticipation, and she noticed the same sounds coming from her own mouth. Obsessed with lust, she tasted his lips, let her mind follow his hands, and just as she thought about how he'd feel inside her, she found the strength to stop.

Quickly turning away so he couldn't see her own pained expression, she waited to hear what he had to say for himself. It took a few moments of tension-filled silence before he spoke.

"How did you figure it out? When?"

"Oh, you had me fooled until a few minutes ago. Then you spoke your sister's pet name, and I remembered looking at a photo of you with her. The one she had on her desk. It was you in your... hmm, I'd say early twenties? No beard but the eyes are the same. And... they've had stories of you in the paper, about your agency and the good work you've done for various firms. Finally, I'm trained FBI. I'm ashamed I didn't pick it up right away. I must be losing my edge."

"Nah! I'm good at playacting, even if I say so myself. You weren't supposed to find out until we had the kids back. In the case that you might need assistance, I'd have stepped forward. I figured if we were linked, I could keep better tabs."

"Linked? Like this? With you coming on to me?"

"God, no. This was never supposed to happen. I just couldn't help myself."

"Yeah? Right. Well, from now on, keep your hands to yourself. The only reason I'm not kicking your sorry ass out of here is because I'll need you to help with Stasia. Those traffickers won't be willing to give up their income easily, and I want them off this island. If I could blast them right out of existence, I would."

"You can't, but I can. And will. I've called a team to come here, and they'll be undercover working the angles. We'll get these bastards, Sophia. I give you my word."

She stared at him and saw the real man, not the vacationing actor standing tall. He meant every word he said, and she believed him. Good. Now she could get busy with the real reason for her trip.

Chapter
Twenty-six

"Barney, why didn't you tell me about Hamilton Alexopoulos passing away? Or about the family barbecue tomorrow?"

"Holy hell, Sophia. I'm sorry. It's been so crazy at the hotel, I've completely lost track of the date. You wouldn't believe it. Right now, Ellie has me running around Old Town organizing fancy tours of the Acropolis and the Grand Palace for a huge party of fun-loving guests from Russia."

Her ears perked up when she heard him mention where his guests came from and his own location. "I'll forgive you if you promise to meet me for a quick Chai tea at Starbucks. My treat."

His voice brightened and agreement followed. "You and your Chai tea. I can be there in twenty minutes – if that works for you?"

"Perfect. See you then."

Sophia turned back to Sam and grinned. "My

cousin is extremely knowledgeable about what goes on in Rhodes. He owns one of the largest villas and spa luxury spots on the Island, so it's in his best interest to be on many of the boards. His place is in a gorgeous spot, close to Tsampika and Lindos."

"It sounds special. If we weren't on this mission, I'd invite you there for the day."

Sophia shrugged and tried to hide her yearning to go to one of her favorite places. "We'll see if maybe we can organize a break before my business on the island is done." She almost blurted out about Barney mentioning his group of Russian visitors but decided to wait until she'd talked with him at the cafe. "By the way, will you stay here with Stasia while I'm gone?"

"Of course. But it's getting a bit boring for her hanging in here at the house. If you promise not to highjack my bike again, I'll take her for a ride to one of the beaches out of town for lunch and a swim. It'll stop her from worrying so much about her predicament. Do you have swimming gear she can wear, maybe a floppy hat so she can hide her appearance on the off chance someone recognizes her?"

"Oh, sure. Yaya has a closetful of clothes we haven't had the time to deal with yet. Stasia can use whatever fits."

"Good. It'll give us something to do while you're gallivanting around town and having fun." He touched the tip of her nose as his way of letting her know he was kidding, and her instinct to rip his finger off never surfaced. In fact, she liked it... too much. Hell, she was beginning to like him too much, and that had to stop. She had a job to do. His next words broke into her thoughts, and she listened.

"You know, since I first arrived and spent a few hours exploring, I wish I could do more. This place is an unfound paradise. It's true, they have cruise ships stopping most days, which brings the numbers of tourists to astronomical levels, but once they depart in the late afternoon, it's heaven. It seems a shame not to get Stasia out and let her see for herself – let some good memories override the ugly ones."

Realizing that Sam's idea had merit, and it was better to amuse the girl rather than letting her wallow in her grief, Sophia quickly agreed. "I guess I can behave and take my car. My own Harley is in the garage and needs some tender loving care before it's good for the road. I wish I had the time to deal with it."

"Give me the keys. I do tender and loving *real* well." He stared into her eyes, and a hot mass of liquid heat drenched her lower groin area, making her clench her muscles. "It'll give me something to do while you're gallivanting with your cousin, drinking lattes and gossiping."

If his audacious wink hadn't followed his

teasing, she might have taken offense at his choice of words. Yeah... no. That wouldn't have happened. She got him, his humor, and his way of making her feel precious.

Chapter Twenty-seven

At Starbuck's, Sophia sat outside under a big green umbrella on the balcony overlooking the cerulean blue water in the distance. The many small sailing ships making their lazy way past the harbor were idyllic, lending a postcard view to one of her new favorite places in the city.

Her hot Chai tea latte tasted heavenly and was her addiction no matter where she happened to be. In minutes, she saw Barney rushing toward her, and she pointed at the second cup waiting at the seat across from hers.

"You look pretty today." Barney leaned over to kiss her cheek before relaxing in his own chair.

"No wonder Ellie thinks you walk on water. When you can spit out compliments like that, you probably get away with murder. How're the kids?

All five of the little monsters?" Sophia loved her nieces and nephew. Considering the youngest was the boy they'd kept trying for, the little hellion knew how to stand up for his place in the pecking order of the female circle surrounding him.

"They're perfect, and so is she. Remember, you promised we could do a cocktail party for you while you're here. Ellie wants to know what night will work best for you?"

"Since the barbecue – the one you forgot to tell me about – is tomorrow, how about the next night? I might be called back to work early, and I'd rather get all my commitments out of the way so I can just laze around for the rest of my time here."

"I'm sure that'll work. Knowing your penchant for keeping things small, she was only inviting the few friends you really care about and not all the rest of the freeloaders who always show up for a good meal. Unfortunately, Corinne and her family are leaving for Europe right after the barbecue, and my sister had to go to Athens for a doctor's appointment. That leaves Yanis, Manos, you me and Ellie."

"Don't go to a lot of trouble for me this time, Barney. I'm really not in a celebrating mood. The fewer the better."

"I hope you won't mind, but Ellie's cousin, Manos Savas, has been here for some time, and she's promised to have him for a meal too. Would you mind if he came to your dinner?"

Giddy, but not wanting to show any reaction, she answered teasingly, "So, you can kill two birds with one stone, right?"

Barney winked. "You got me. That's about it."

"What's this about a Russian party at the hotel? You mentioned them on the phone."

Barney's smile faded and he looked perturbed. Shaking his head to emphasize his next words, he said, "They're loud and showy and expect constant, special attention. I don't know, there's just something about them that gets to me."

"Which part of Russia are they from?"

"Sochi I believe."

The same city where they picked up Stasia and the others. Hmmm. "Are they just men or couples, families, what?"

"Mostly men, but a few have women with them, young, pretty but very unhappy women. I'm glad they're only here for a week. It makes me nervous to see the men drinking in the bar and then acting like juveniles with those females. It's not my place to question them, but I have to admit a few of the females look at me with such sad eyes, it's hard not to step in."

"What line of work are the men in?"

"I don't know. They certainly aren't scholars. And they're loud and disrupt the rest of the guests. But they have money and expect the best, so who am I to question?"

As Barney sipped his latte, Sophia's mind

wondered about what Barney told her until she noticed a problem below them on the sidewalk. A man was hollering at his three kids and one of the smaller of the girls had decided to push his buttons. The little imp had her hands on her hips, her bottom lip puckered, and her sharp negative headshaking told the story that she was refusing to budge. The others were doing as they were told and getting into the car, but not her. She obviously had a mind of her own.

Seeing herself in the little one's behavior, she was intrigued. Her Yaya would have handled her refusal by making a deal with her. She had a way of coming up with something Sophia wanted more than getting her own way – like a movie night with popcorn or a swim together at the beach.

But this man was nothing like her grandmother. His beet-red, sweaty face and ugly expression portrayed someone on the edge of losing his temper. He grabbed for the child's arm, but quick as a rascal, she stepped away, looking scared, but standing her ground.

Sophia stood and ignored Barney's warning not to interfere and then his sigh of resignation. She went down the stairs to where the scene had brought other looky-loos to see what all the noise was about, and they now had a crowd. The child, loving the limelight, had begun letting him have it with both barrels. "You can't tell me what to do. You're not my daddy. I want Mummy."

At his wit's end, the frantic male lunged unexpectedly, scooped her up and had a battle on his hands. Not only did the little one put up a fight, she wriggled so maniacally, his grip loosened, and she'd have fallen off his shoulder if Sophia hadn't been there to snatch her out of the air before she hit the gravel.

"Goddammit, Marion, stop being a brat!" Those were the words he yelled just as she broke loose.

Safe in Sophia's arms, the child now crying hysterically started screaming back at him. "My name's May, not... not Marion. I want my mummy."

Sophia hugged her close and patted her back. She looked at the man barely holding it together and bit out one word that let everyone know she was now in control. "Explain."

Sensing he stood before someone with authority, he fell back against the car and wiped his face with shaking hands. "Thank God you caught her. She's a real monster, but I wouldn't want her to have fallen."

"Yet you purposely grabbed her so hard, she now has bruises forming." Sophia had been rubbing the child's back and noticed the discoloration beginning to appear on the preschooler's arms. "Where's her mother?"

Everyone surrounding them could hear the child's cries for her mother. The oldest, who had gotten into the car, backed out and came over to where May still clung to Sophia, her drenched face hidden against her shoulder.

She began commiserating with her sister in a sweet way before answering Sophia's questions. "Mom stayed at the hotel. She's sick, and Rex said he'd take us for ice cream so she could rest. He's her boyfriend, but he's being mean, yelling at us all the time. We just want to go back to Mom."

Angry at being the bad guy in the picture, Rex snarled, "I'm not being mean. You kids never listen. When a person tells you to do something, you do it. You don't have to argue every single, goddamn time."

Sophia growled, "Watch it, buddy. I think you need a break. Which hotel are you staying at? I'll take the kids back to their mom."

When he named Barney's place, Sophia looked at her cousin who had just joined in the throng as an interested bystander and angled her head questioningly. He stepped forward. "Mr. Drew, you seem to be having a bad time here."

Recognizing Barney from the hotel, the fellow shrunk like a full balloon untied and slumped down even more. "Hi, Barney. Look, I'm not feeling well at all. It's the heat I guess, but I can't deal with these kids. Can you grab them a taxi to take them back to the hotel? I need some time to get my shit together. And that little devil is too much for me to handle right now."

Barney stepped closer, bent to wave the other child in the car to come over to him and corralled the older one by Sophia before he shot her a look that called her an interfering busybody. He gently put his arm around their shoulders and calmly agreed, "They can have their ice cream here with my cousin and me. Then I'm heading home after we have our visit and can take them to the hotel. They'll be fine."

He looked at the two oldest and asked, "Would you like to come back with me to the hotel?"

"Yes, sir. Please." Both the boy and the girl nodded enthusiastically.

Barney turned back to face the suddenly satisfied man. "Mr. Drew, l—"

Obviously trying to be cordial now that he'd passed on his responsibilities, he turned friendly. "Not mister, Barney. Call me Rex."

"Okay then, Rex. These kids and their mom are welcome at the hotel, but I think you need to find yourself another place to stay."

"Barney—"

"You better do as Barney says," Sophia cut in. "He doesn't get mad very often, but you've just pushed his pissed button. If you don't want to see him really angry, move out."

She turned her back and didn't see the middle finger he threw her way. But Barney did. His warning came out in a menacing tone Sophia had never heard him use before. "Look man, she's FBI and doesn't suffer fools easily. You really don't want to mess with her."

The murmur from the crowd covered his reply as Sophia and Barney ushered the kids back upstairs and inside to the counter. While they chose their favorite ice creams and desserts, Sophia ordered two more Chai teas so her and Barney could resume their discussion.

Seated with the kids at the table next to them, happily eating their treats, Sophia looked at Barney and said, "What?"

"You never cease to amaze me. From the time we were kids, you always had to stick up for the underdog."

"Makes me a good agent."

"Makes you a great person. I love you, cuz, but you do know you've just saddled me with three kids on my one afternoon off."

"And you adore kids, so don't try messing with me. Now tell me about this Manos character."

Looking slightly shocked, Barney said, "what do you want to know?"

"Everything. I've heard his name mentioned twice since I got here a few days ago, and he seems to have everyone in a tizzy that he brought his kids here for the summer."

Barney looked pained, but he sipped his drink then whispered, "He's a pain in the ass if you ask me. But Ellie cares about him – seems they have a history from when they grew up. She wants me to give him the benefit of the doubt."

"What's the doubt?"

"That he's an asshole. Really, Soph, he acts like he's king of the mountain. And since he's come back, he's building his place into an armed compound with guards for chrissakes. We dropped by last weekend, Ellie wanted to take him a new batch of olives we'd just jarred, and he strutted around the place like he had a stick up his arse. And, his kids are afraid of him."

"Kids?"

"Yeah, he has his three kids there with him, and they all cower around the creep. Makes me sick."

"Three?"

Chapter Twenty-eigh
t

All the way back to the house, Sophia rethought Barney's words. How the hell did Manos have three kids with him when she knew for a fact that Maureen and him only had a set of five-year-old twins? Where did the third kid come from?

And why did her case suddenly get so convoluted? It was one thing to snatch a couple of kids back from a father who stole them from their American mother. It was a completely different scenario when the father was partnered with Russians in a vicious smuggling operation.

And from the way Barney described his guests, she wondered if the Russians at his hotel were somehow tied to the trafficking the city had begun dealing in? And Manos was involved in the whole goddamn mess.

On the way back to Yaya's house, Bill Bruner called through on the car phone, and she had to squash her first inclination of ignoring the call.

"Hey, boss, what's up?" Knowing the ASAC would pick up on her tone, she purposely used teasing to cover up her worry.

"You okay, brat?"

He was alone or he'd never have used those words. Good, she could let him in on the situation, and he could get her some answers. "Yep. All set up for a meeting tomorrow with Manos Savas at a family barbecue, and Barney's having both of us to a dinner at his hotel the next night. He's my cousin's wife's cousin."

"He's your cousin's... what the fuck? Never mind. Just tell me what you need. I can hear it in your voice that you're ready to drop something on me."

"Yep. I am. Barney just told me that Savas has three kids with him at his compound, and they're supposedly all his."

"What? Compound? Three kids? Are you losing it, kiddo?"

"Call me that again Bunny, and I let loose with your nickname in the coffee room."

A thick chuckle broke through and a ground out cuss word before he answered, "Don't you dare blackmail me cause I still have that baby picture of you with your gigantic stuffed grumpy cat. The one where it's hard to tell which is chubbier, you or the cat."

"Not that threat again. I keep telling you, no one can prove it's me."

"Proof isn't necessary if I tell them. Think anyone's going to argue with me?"

Backing down like they both knew would happen, she giggled and replied, "Okay, okay. Sir Boss, can you get me everything there is on Manos's background – if he was married before, mistresses, whatever? Barney said this kid was around nine or ten and his name is Alexandro. And Bill, there's some shit happening here on the island that I kind of got involved in."

A raspy groan sounded before he said, "What is it this time?"

"I rescued a girl called Anastasia Dedov from her Russian pimps the other night, and she's not alone. She was brought over in a shipping container from Sochi along with a dozen or so more just like her. They're trafficking here too, Bill, and it makes me sick. The old mayor's death is suspicious, to say the least, and they now have a new mayor and police commander to cover up all the dirty, underhanded bullshit going on."

"Ooo-kay. That sounds too dangerous for you to get mixed up in, Sophia. I mean it. Snatch the twins and get the hell out of there. We'll get to Manos later when he tries to get back into the country to steal his kids again."

"Who's to say he won't send someone else.

Look, I met a man you'll approve of who's helping me with this case. We'll be fine, and I'll get back as soon as I can. Just get me that info I need."

"Not until you tell me who this character is?"

"Fine. Have you ever met the governor's brother?"

"Sam Reagan? You mean the bigshot, private muscle with a good rep and a whole hell of a lot of influence?"

"Bingo!"

Chapter
Twenty-nine

Sam enjoyed watching Stasia slip back into being a young girl having fun. Here at the sandy beach full of sun-lovers and people enjoying life, she bloomed and seemed to forget her troubles. He purposely chose a spot towards the end of a sandy slope where they had privacy.

On their way, he'd stopped at a shop and rented some high-class snorkeling gear for the day. He wanted to give the unhappy girl an experience of doing something he loved to do whenever he got the chance. Taking her out into the silky turquoise water in the small, enclosed bay would be a good memory of her time here. Something she might think of when she looked back.

There were millions of tiny fish circling them, and even a few larger species who seemed to accept they weren't a danger. Stasia excitedly pointed out every underwater feature as they swam past, and he got a kick out of giving her the special memory.

After spending an hour or so in the water, they soaked up the sun, drying off. Sam handed her his expensive, top-of-the-line phone and watched her tune in music on YouTube while he opened his iPad and did some work.

After they had their fill of the extreme heat, he led her to the beach's only restaurant, which was really just a large, colorful hut-styled building with a huge awning surrounding it and many covered tables. There were a lot of people there, which made Stasia decide to wear her glasses and her hat.

It was while they were ordering lamb souvlaki lunches that her name rang out from a fat man on his way past. "Stasia? Is this you?"

Sam stood to block her and said in a friendly way, "No, my sister's name is Maisie. You must have mistaken her for another girl."

The idiot, too stupid to sense danger, stepped around Sam and pointed. His Russian accent drew interest. "It's Stasia. One of the girls I met at the hotel—"

"It isn't." Sam seeing Stasia's face pale, and a sickly expression appear, again drew the attention of the blustering fool. This time his tone was anything but friendly. His snapping out words should have been understood by even the densest jerk. That's if they hadn't imbibed so many beers, he could smell their breath from a foot away.

"Back off, man. We're having lunch, and you're embarrassing her."

Finally, sensing the trouble he was in, fatso started to stumble away. A lack of intelligence stopped him. He pointed a finger as if he had one last comment to make.

The bastard didn't know what hit him.

A while later, packing up their gear, Stasia said yet again, "you shouldn't have made him walk like that, twisting his arm. I thought they'd call the police."

"Chubby had it coming. And the rest of the customers agreed."

"Yes. And the lunch was delicious. Truthfully, the whole day has been wonderful. Thank you, Sam."

Chapter Thirty

The barbecue was held on Corinne's sprawling property about twenty kilometers outside the city. Sophia arrived just as the others were setting up the tables in the garden. Many people milled around in groups, catching up with friends, while an even bigger cluster of kids played in the olive grove with the dogs. Bird sounds echoed through the air letting everyone know their feathered-friends were upset with the unusual disturbance.

It was a lovely family scene that at any other time Sophia would enjoy, but the undercurrents were too crucial for her to really relax. First, she was greeted by Corinne, who tried picking her brain about Sam.

"Tell me more about the hunkster you were with when I ran into you on Wednesday. What a specimen of male hunkiness!"

"Hunkster, hunkiness? What are you, a

teenager? You're a married woman, my friend. For shame. What would your Eric say if he heard you rhapsodize about some guy in the marketplace?"

"He wasn't just some guy, Sophia. And you know it. You had smitten plastered all over your face."

"Plastered, yes. Because of him? I beg to differ. I was ahh... smitten by the ouzo."

Laughing, enjoying the repartee, Corinne pushed, "Sure, sure. You can fool yourself, but I saw the look on his face, and my name isn't Genius if he hasn't contacted you again by now." She laughed when Sophia couldn't hide the truth from her expression. A little humored, somewhat floored, but a whole lot pissed, she grudgingly admitted, "So what? He's an American military guy on leave. We spent some time together. No biggie!"

Before Corinne had a chance to tease her more, Ellie, Barney and the kids arrived in bulk. The noise level ascended shockingly when all four little females saw Sophia. Giggling screeches highlighted their excitement. They tried getting to her, but their spoiled family charmer, little Bruce, hit her open arms first, and then it was a free for all.

It was almost an hour before she broke loose from the kids, but not before she made them introduce her to the twins who were quietly standing on the outskirts of the gang involved in a fun game of soccer.

"Jack, don't you want to play ball with the other boys? They'll let you if you want." She felt sorry for the small five-year-old who looked dejected.

Before Jack could answer, another boy stepped out of the game and broke into their conversation. "Baby's scared to get hurt. He never wants to do nothing."

This kid had an attitude of insolence that annoyed Sophia, so she turned with a straight face and a warning tone, "It's not nice to call someone names."

"I can. He's my brother... my half-brother, and he's a baby."

"How old are you?"

"I'm nine." The skinny braggart stuck out his chest, and his disrespectful tone had her bile rising. *Little shit!*

Then she pointed at Jack and asked, "And how old is he?"

His twin sister, Casey, stepped forward and yelled, "He's only five. Like me. I'm five, and those kids are mean. They play rough, and we don't want to play with them anyway."

Sophia saw that Barney's bunch had come to see what all the hoopla was about. She caught Bruce's eye and waved him over. "Here's a little gentleman you're age who will play with you. Him and his sisters like to play tag, so maybe it's best if you go with them." She watched as Jack and Casey ran away happily with Barney's gang and turned to see a sneering grin on the rougher kid's face.

She had to ask, "Who's your papa?"

A man stepped into view just then. "I am. Go play, Alexandro." Manos Savas held out his hand while his handsome face broke into a smile that would normally have attracted. But knowing what she did about the creep, it just made her wish there were wide steel bars in front of his overly large white smile.

"I'm Manos Savas. Alexandro is my oldest son. Also, the twins you were so kind to, Jack and Casey, are my children. I've brought them to Rodos to live with me after their mama left us."

You prick! That's the story you're telling everyone so you can gain sympathy and get accepted?

Deciding to play along, Sophia accepted his handshake and added, "She must be a fool."

Once they'd introduced themselves, Manos followed her around like a hound dog for the rest of the day. Every time she looked at the tall, dark-haired man with his coiffured waves that must take time every morning to arrange just so, and the insolent swagger that showed his self-love, she'd swallow her distaste. Knowing what she knew about him, she had a hard time not shoving his overly large smiling white gleamers down his throat.

All the while she visited with her Yaya's older friends and caught up with Ellie and the cousins, he wouldn't leave her side. When Barney reminded her of the dinner party the next night, Manos lit up and said he'd had some friends show up in Rhodes, staying at Barney's place, and had thought to cancel, but now nothing would force him to miss an evening in her company.

"I'll look forward to it then." She smiled her fakest smile and grinned when Barney made a gagging face only she could see.

Corinne broke into their conversation saying they were ready for the shooting contest and most of the guests headed in the direction she pointed. They went toward the back where the property overlooked the gorgeous distant views of the old town, and then the ocean behind. This is where they'd set up a few activities for their guests, but the one that garnered the most attention was the shooting contest that Sophia would normally have entered.

Not wanting to stay longer than necessary, she decided not to take the first prize away from the second-best marksman in her family, Barney. Seeing as how most of the guests were over at the shooting grounds, she decided to make her goodbyes to the elders on the porch when Ellie approached with a serious look on her pretty face. A look that meant business.

"Barney sent me to get you."

"Why? What's up?"

"My cousin, Manos, the big show-off, is winning the contest and has suggested a wager on the final round that Barney doesn't want to take." She reiterated, "He sent me to get you."

"To do what exactly?"

"You know what. He's always known you're the better shot and can win. And he wants Manos beaten so bad, it's written all over him."

"He'd never be so insensitive that he'd let it show. You know that, Ellie."

"Maybe. But I know him, and it's all he can do not to wrap the rifle around Manos's bragging neck. I've never known my cousin to be such a jerk. He deserves to lose. Will you come?"

Sophia hesitated.

"Please. For Barney."

"Well if you're going to put it that way, of course." She followed Ellie back to the crowd at the far end of the yard where Eric had set up a shooting range very much like one would see at the Olympics. Marksmen aimed at targets at distances of ten, twenty-five, and fifty meters and the best shooter won the round.

Barney and Manos were now competing at the furthest targets. They both used gleaming, fairly new .22 rifles with quality sights. Sophia could see at a glance they'd been cleaned and well taken care of. In fact, they were better rifles than what one might expect at most competitions, and she understood that if faulty equipment wasn't the reason why Barney was losing, it had to be that Manos was a better shot.

Which would explain why he wanted her to enter. When it came to winning, she'd always beaten him in the past. And from the look on his determined red-faced expression, plus the fact that he couldn't resist a challenge, he wanted to put Manos in his place more than he wanted it to be him who did the putting.

As she walked through the crowd, relatives and people who had seen her prowess and were glad she'd shown up, muttered phrases like, "go get him, honey" and "now we'll see some shooting."

In time to hear Manos throw down the gauntlet, she had to hide her distaste and pretend not to be sickened by his egotistical behavior while he tormented Barney. "Come on you wuss, let's make the bet two hundred euros. What do you say?"

"That's too steep, Manos. It's a friendly competition." Barney, who was notorious at being a spendthrift, wore a horrified expression.

"Okay, then, one hundred euros." Manos took out his bulging money clip, counted five twenties and forced them into Ellie's hand. "Here, honey. You hold the money, but don't put it away, cause I'll be taking it right back along with Barney's donation in a few minutes."

As soon as Barney saw that Sophia had returned with Ellie, his smile grew, he winked her way and said, "I'll take the bet on one condition – Sophia gets to shoot this round for me."

Stunned, Manos looked from Barney to her, and

then back at his competitor. "You want her to be the one to take the defeat. That's not very kind of you, Barney."

Sophia, wincing at the disgusted tone that Manos accused Barney with, decided it was time to put an end to the foolishness. "Okay, how about I take the bet, winner take all, and we shoot two out of three to give you a bit of a chance."

Manos, not liking her tone nor her challenge looked around the cheering group and shrugged. "Fine with me, but instead of you paying, promise me you'll have dinner with me and my children at my home."

Crapola! Now it suddenly dawned on her that if she beat him in front of everyone and took his money, he might lose interest in her, and she'd be up the creek trying to get close.

Yet losing to him would be impossible for her to live with.

Son of a bitch!

Chapter Thirty-one

The first round he won easily as she intended. He might be a good shooter, but she knew instantly, she was better.

He stepped further back, as if he meant to give her more odds, and she followed.

"No, you stay closer, dear Sophia. It'll give you more of a chance."

Gritting her teeth, losing her cool, she instantly raised the rifle and barely taking aim, she shot the target, getting a bullseye. Then she turned back to stare him down, her ire awakened.

His eyes met hers, a shocked expression suddenly appearing. Now he understood that she could shoot... she really was competition.

Seeing as how he'd already made the move backwards and couldn't renege on his gloating action, he lifted the rifle very seriously and took his time, but he didn't come close to her fantastic shot.

Pretending to be overly confident, she backed up to stand next to him and lifted the rifle. She saw Barney's smile and knew she had to do something to end things before she regretted what her heart urged her to do, but her brain argued she couldn't.

Slowly, lowering the rifle, she turned to Manos and grinned cheekily. "You know, I'm not going to take this next shot. We'll never know who's better, and it doesn't matter really. I want to have dinner with you, so let's just call it a tie."

Close enough to see the relief before he hid it, his big-mouthed smile broke out, and he passed his gun over to Eric. "You're right, my love." Acting the gentleman, he added, "I'd never have made you lose in front of all these people. It wouldn't be right."

Once the crowd dispersed, grumbling about the outcome, she craved to get out of there and began earnestly saying her goodbyes. First, she dealt with Barney, whose look said he'd get an explanation, and if he had to, he'd wait. Corinne and the others were next, and hugs plus promises to see them next time she visited were shared with them all.

She turned to a hovering Manos, hoping he couldn't read the searing dislike she covered up with fake interest. He walked her to her car and opened her door, saying, "I wish we'd had more time together."

"I'm sorry, but I must leave. I, too, have friends here on the island and promised to have them for dinner."

"I feel like we've only just met. I have so many questions for you. Barney said you work for the government in Washington, and that you're single but dedicated to your job."

"So, you asked about me. I'm flattered." Thanking God for Barney's reticence of keeping information to a need-to-know-basis, she added, "I'm a bit of a workaholic. We can learn more about each other tomorrow at Ellie's place." Looking away from him, she pointed behind him. "Your little ones are looking very tired and probably need to rest, and I really must leave now." *Before I puke all over your showy white silk shirt.*

He made a disparaging wave at the kids. "Those two are always dragging themselves around. They miss their bitch of a mother. But you're right. It's time also for me to leave. Until tomorrow." Before she could snatch back her hand, he put it to his mouth to leave a kiss there and didn't know how bloody lucky he was that she didn't follow through on the punch she visualized.

Slimy bastard!

Chapter Thirty-two

Arriving at home, Sophia interrupted a game of cards between Stasia and Sam. The normality of their scene made her want to shower off Manos's scent.

Stasia smiled her welcome and asked, "How was this barbecue? Did you see many of your family members?"

"Yes, quite a few were there. It was fun. Especially being with my cousin's family. He has five young children, and they like a lot of attention. Ellie can't keep a nanny longer than a week because they wear the poor women out as fast as she hires them. Since I see them so seldom, an hour of their energy is a treat."

"They're lucky to have cousin like you. I'm oldest of large family. I know what it's like to deal with bunch of children. I miss them very much. I wished—" She stopped talking and waved her hand as if to shut off her thoughts. "Never mind. If it's okay, I think I lay down for a while. Too much sun."

"Of course, it's okay. You don't need permission."

After watching the hunch-backed teenager let the swinging door close behind her, Sophia joined Sam at the table and questioned him with a look he understood. "She misses her family and feels bad about her promise to help her father financially. She's also worried about the others at the Rhodes house and whether we'll be able to get her passport back for her."

He reached to the counter nearby for a mug and offered her a cup of coffee he'd just brewed. "How did it go? Was arsehole there?"

"Yes. And that's the perfect title for him. I kind of expected not to like the man, knowing what I do about him, but he's an even bigger creep than I envisioned. Although he did invite me to have dinner with him at his place, and in two days, which is what I was aiming for. While I'm there, I intend to offer to take the little ones off his hands for the day. I'll beg to take them to a fair and magic show they're going to be advertising in Marmaris."

"That's in Turkey."

"Yes. They have day excursions to the city advertised by many boats on the pier. I'm going to talk him into letting me take the twins to the circus the day after our dinner."

"Is there a circus?"

"No. But I can organize a poster to be made that'll make him think it's legit."

"I can take care of that. I have a guy who can do anything with a computer." A smile began to form on Sam's face. "Manos will have to give over their passports for you to be able to take them into another country, right?"

"Exactly. I'll book flights from there as soon as we arrive and have them back in their mama's arms before he even realizes we aren't returning. My only problem is making sure his other son, Alexandro, doesn't want to join us. I'll need to make the poster look babyish with clowns and pony rides, etc. That way, he might refuse and papa will listen because anyone can see he dotes on the boy much more so than he does on the twins."

"According to Maureen, he's always made out as if he adores them, but she's seen instances where the kids are afraid of his temper and often turn to her rather than him."

"I saw that today. They looked unhappy, and he said they missed their bi... ahh, mother."

His look hardened when she bit off the word they both knew Manos had used instead. Sam actually growled his comeback. "Not nearly as much as—"

Suddenly, Barney's special ringtone sounded, and his face appeared on her phone's screen. Sam stopped what he was saying, waiting for her to answer.

Intending on standing and taking the phone out of the room, she stumbled on the table leg and had to sit back down. "I can explain, Barney. Don't freak out."

"You didn't take the shot. Everyone knew you'd have won. Chrissakes, after your little snit shot, he knew it too, but couldn't believe it. What the hell, Soph?"

"Calm down, cuz. I couldn't beat him and still keep his interest. He's not the kind of man who would take losing easily and still want to be with the woman who made him look bad. And though I can't discuss a case with you, he's part of why I'm really here."

Silence rang in the room while Barney digested her words. Then in a much calmer tone, he backed off and apologized. "Damn, Soph, I'm sorry. I should have known you'd have your reasons. Look, I know you can't talk about an ongoing case, but can you promise to tell me more about it once it's settled? I really want to know he's gotten what he deserves. Even Ellie was disgusted at how he's changed, and she's sorry we have to put up with his company tomorrow at dinner." A mean-sounding snarl followed. "Don't know how my fist won't be finding its way into his smug face."

Laughing, Sophia answered, "Now you know how I felt all day. You promise to behave, and I'll catch you up on everything after the fact. See you tomorrow."

Having forgotten that Sam heard every word because of Barney's loud voice, she jumped when he added, "I like your Barney, and I've never met him."

Grudgingly, she admitted, "He'd like you too."

Leaning toward her before she could escape, imprisoning her face between his large, gentle hands, he kissed her swiftly and brazenly added, "As much as *you* like me?"

She stared at him, keeping her face from showing any expression. Then she said, "Who says I like you?"

"You'll like me more when I tell you the gang arrived today, and they're at an Airbnb near Old Town. We're meeting tonight to organize the take-down of the house."

"What? You found it? How?"

"I told you, I have a guy who's a whiz on the computer. He's done a Google search of the properties within the distance that Stasia said they drove to the hotel the night you met – exactly ten minutes. Then he used her description of the fields around the house until he found a few examples, sent them to me, and Stasia was able to pick out the two she thought might be the ones. We set up surveillance at both and sure enough, she'd nailed it. One of the houses has a whole bunch of young people living there. And, we know exactly where it's situated."

Glowing from his news, Sophia jumped to her feet, her energy suddenly activated. "What are we waiting for. Let me change, and I'm your girl."

Sam's voice followed her to the door, and before she left the room, she heard him say, "that's right, sweetheart, you are mine. Glad you're getting used to the idea."

She almost stopped to set him right, but couldn't because of the silly grin on her face and the warm glow suddenly activated in her heart.

Chapter
Thirty-three

Once outside, he led her to her own bike rather than his, and she was shocked to see the striking Harley gleaming from being freshly washed. It looked wonderful, and she couldn't wait to take it out.

"Will you ride with me driving?" She asked him reluctantly.

"Only if I'm blind."

"Boy-o, no one else has ever driven my bike."

"Fine, we take mine." He stood his ground and waited for her next move.

She walked toward his vehicle and at the last minute, swerved to hers. "The clutch sticks a bit."

"I know. Who do you think filled the gas tank?" She shoved his arm in a joking way and muttered, "just get on."

It wasn't so bad riding behind Sam on her two-up seat, the one she'd used for taking Yaya with her since her grandmother couldn't drive her own Sportster super-low anymore. In fact, she loved it. Her top-of-the-line Harley Davidson Softail Deluxe had more power than the ones Sam rented, and they rode comfortably together.

Holding on to him, she didn't mind that it wasn't her in front. In her way of thinking, his macho stance on being in control was understandable. There weren't a lot of men that she'd put up with their nonsense of 'me man, me in charge'. But from him, she accepted his truth. The man led and others followed. Some guys were born to lead.

They arrived on Kennenti – a narrow street where both sides were filled with nice-looking homes and the road with parked cars. Old-growth trees over-looked the noticeably cracked sidewalks and lent an appearance of dark tranquility. Sam pulled into a driveway opening to a narrow side street and parked.

They rang the bell at the door. Within a few minutes a huge giant with longish hair to match his bushy beard and wearing a big smile opened to them and ushered them straight through to the apartment on the main floor.

"Hey big guy." Sam greeted the other man with a side hug and slapped his back, while Sophia watched two other people close in. Both were good-looking. Both had frames that screamed they were physically fit. And both wore huge grins at the sight of their boss.

Once he'd greeted them with affectionate hugs, they turned to her. She held out her hand to the approaching female first. "Sophia Dunne."

"Anne Carmen, pleased to meet you, Special Agent." Checking the slim, tall woman with short, dark-blonde hair, blue eyes, and a gorgeous smile to see if there was any animosity because of her police role and seeing none, she nodded and answered, "same here."

Then she took turns shaking hands with the other two that Anne introduced. Marc, the hulk who'd met them at the door, came forward first. His searing gaze stripped her of any pretense, and she gave back as good as she got. When his good-looking face broke into a smile of welcome, she had no choice but for hers to do the same.

Next, Anne pointed to the man known as David, and her face softened. He was a kid really, but one most females would have felt an instant attraction to. Holy shit, what a looker. At least six-four with intense blue eyes and thick dark hair worn longer on the top.

He had a smile one could sink into, and he held her hand far longer than good etiquette demanded. He dove into her eyes as if he needed to read her, and then ensnared her under his spell. Never having had an experience quite like this before, rattled and not wanting to make a scene, she gave him a few seconds to stare his fill before she winked and turned away. His huge grin let her see him for the young man he really was, but whoa... he could flirt with the angels and they'd fall in love.

She followed the others past a large table they'd set up as their main office area. Glancing around, she liked the look of the place. It was spacious, modern, and comfortable.

The large inviting balcony behind the full wall of windows where they'd left half-empty beer bottles to come and greet their boss was where they all headed back to. The big guy who met them at the door, Marc, offered her a drink and she accepted a Corona, as did Sam.

Once they were all seated outside, with the constant breeze cooling off the heat from the fading sun, they passed around the numerous bowls filled with chips and popcorn and joked about their trip and how much they wanted some personal time to enjoy the city.

Sam gave them a few minutes to rave about their location, the bakery shop a minute away from the house, the local restaurant on the corner with great food and the closeness of the medieval castle. Then he shut down their enthusing and opened the real discussion. "Okay, okay. We'll talk about time off once we get this case under control." Becoming serious, he asked the questions Sophia wanted answers for.

"Dave, did you get all the surveillance info from John-john? The location of the house, how many are staying there and the number of guards they've placed around the property?"

Serious now, laptop in front of him, Dave answered, "Yeah. I've uploaded everything to the computer I have here. As you know, Marc and Anne did a drive-by earlier and vouched it was the right place."

Anne added, "Just as we got there, they were loading the girls into the vans." She opened her phone and showed the photographs she'd taken while they surveilled the house. The pictures illustrated a majority of young girls, some very young. Heart aching at seeing the proof and being able to put faces to the actual sufferers, Sophia also counted three males.

Anne broke into her visualizations, pulling her back to the balcony. "I counted fifteen and most were young, one couldn't have been more than twelve. We followed them to three bars where they must have them working. One van left and headed up the highway to Lindos. David watched it on Google, and it stopped at a sleazy place not far from the ritzy spa hotel your cousin owns." Anne aimed the last part of her remark toward Sophia.

Not surprised they'd looked into her background, Sophia thought out loud. "Could be those Russian tourists staying at Barney's hotel want some extra services. They'd know the girls wouldn't be allowed at Barney's, so they're setting them up in a place close by. Bastards!"

Anne grinned her agreement and turned to Sam

while he gave orders. "When we move in, I want that place shut down and their captives freed. Not only that, I want you to look everywhere to find their personal papers. They'll all need their passports before they can be sent back to their homes."

"What if those documents aren't kept in the residence? What if Manos or one of the others in charge has them at his place?"

"So far, from what we've been able to put together, there are three top men involved right here in Rhodes – the new mayor, the police commander, and Manos."

David cut in here and added, "Manos looks to be the boss if all the documents we've managed to intercept are any indication. He's calling the shots here, and it looks like he's setting up business in the States. They have a ship arriving at a location on the eastern seaboard in five days, leaving from the same port as the one that brought these victims to Greece. Seems they're expanding their operations."

Sophia's ears perked up and she questioned, "Whereabouts on the eastern seaboard? I'll need to inform my boss."

"The Department of Homeland Security has an Arrival Notification system that says they'll show up in the Port of New York and New Jersey at one of their six terminals. I'll let John-john deal with that mess. He'll keep us appraised."

Sophia stood and leaned over so she could be closer to Sam who sat at the head of the table. "I want any information you have to be passed over to my boss ASAC Bruner at the FBI headquarters in Washington. Can that be put in place? He'll want to be kept in the loop, especially since he was the one who became involved with Maureen and Manos in the first place. Plus, any assistance you might need from the local authorities, he can arrange."

"Will do. I'll contact him about our systems and get him involved. Right now, since that ship's still at sea, we need to solve this matter about the trafficking here in Greece."

"You mean in Rhodes." Sophia had a bad feeling about his answer. She knew the assholes wouldn't make a huge pile of money by having just one house filled with captives working for them. Now that she understood the size of the operation and how long they'd possibly been at their dirty business, there had to be more... a lot more.

Sam looked at her, the seriousness of his expression had her heart dropping. She'd hit the fucking nail on the head. There were more places.

"You've already figured it out, Sophia. We know of at least five other houses in different areas of Greece: two in Athens, one each in Crete, Santorini, and Mykonos. From the hundreds of millions of dollars John-john has managed to scope out hidden in various accounts, money Manos and his partners have accumulated over the four years they've been in business, they've had to not only increase their numbers but move to different locations to earn that kind of moolah."

"Then you know who he's working with? It can't be a one-man operation."

"I do, yes. We've delved into his background with a fine-tooth comb and found the people he has working for him on all the other islands and in Athens. He also has a firm of questionable bankers laundering the money into real estate in the U.S. for him."

"Do you know where these other houses are?"

"We know of the ones in Athens. I have two men watching his partners there. We just found his property in Santorini and we're closing in on the one in Mykonos. I'll have that location by tomorrow."

"Gentle Jesus, the man's worse than I envisioned, and I already had him sized up as lower than a mud-covered slug."

Joining in with the laughter all around, Sam agreed with her estimation and then added, "From what John-john has been able to put together, the slimeball first gathered investors on some crazy scheme for tourism in Greece and used that money to fund his set-up. And he was able to get to those wealthy stakeholders through my sister's connections."

"Whoa. So, now it's personal."

"You bet your sweet ass it's personal. I'll not stand by and see him continue with his dirty business when I can put a stop to it."

"I'd never expect you to. Right now, my job is to get the twins away from Manos and back home to their mother. As much as I'd love to be in on whatever you're organizing to bring the prick down," she looked around to all the others at the table, "I can't be seen to have anything to do with it. Just know, I care as much about Stasia and her friends as anyone. If I'm to get any sleep in the next few days, I need to be updated with whatever is happening."

"Oh, don't you worry. We won't be making any moves until you're safely on your way back to the States with Jack and Casey. Then we'll hit all the places at once. And you'll be the first to know what's taking place."

***

Sam couldn't believe how happy it made him to think about Sophia safe and out of the way of the shit he knew would be going down when they made their move on the house. Men who were willing to turn youngsters into slave laborers and make them do the horrific kinds of things these hostages were made to do wouldn't sit back easily and let it all be whisked away.

He'd taken steps on the other islands and in Athens to find men who were legit, men of integrity willing to help put a stop to the crap in their countries. He'd withheld the final info about the locations of the houses and would share them all at the same time so the operations would take place simultaneously as soon as Sophia and the kids were free.

He loved his niece and nephew. And the thought of them being unhappy or worse yet, injured in any way, made him ill. But just thinking about anything happening to his silver-haired beauty made the world instantly turn into a black void of pain.

A place where he wouldn't want to exist without her. How the hell he'd let his feelings become so invested, he couldn't say. Maybe it was the warmth of her body behind him while riding the motorcycle. Her chuckling when he took a fast hill or a wild curve.

Or maybe it was her eyes so guarded, often cold, and seldom welcoming. Until he snuck under her guard and put his hands and lips on her.

Then he saw the wildness, the heat, and deep, deep inside her, he felt the glorious affection of a woman who would be a faithful champion forever. This girl wouldn't give her devotion easily, but when she did, my God, she'd mean it from the bottom of her very soul.

By accident, looking for a pen at her house, he'd found some of the notes she'd sent to her Yaya. Her declarations of love and tenderness, how much she missed not being there with the older woman, and how very much her Yaya meant to her.

If he was ever lucky enough to win a place in her heart like her grandmother, then hell... he'd be the luckiest man alive. Considering they didn't have a lot of time left in this paradise to learn about each other, he would be using every precious second he had to get her feeling the same way about him... starting tonight.

Chapter
Thirty-four

Tonight, they had a full moon and it seemed such a shame to waste it. Sam drove the bike to a hill overlooking the bay and pulled to a stop. Before they'd left the others, he'd grabbed a couple bottles of cold beer and passed one over to her now.

He watched as she walked closer to the cliff and saw her illuminated by the huge ball of yellowy-white magic behind her. If he could store this precious moment in his heart forever, he would. Thinking fast, he slipped his phone from his pocket and quickly snapped a shot and then looked to see what showed up.

There in his screen stood a tall woman with shiny silver hair gently wafting around her shoulders. Her leather pants fit her slim body like a glove as did her light-weight black jacket that gleamed from good leather. A white T-shirt set off the breasts he ached to touch. If he could lay her down on the grass and have his way with her, he'd know he'd died and gone to heaven.

She turned and grinned. "I can feel your thoughts from here. You have a dirty mind."

He laughed. "It's not dirty if a guy has... has affections for the woman he's imagining doing dirty things to."

She laughed as he'd hoped she would. "You're incorrigible, boy-o. I'm not going to indulge you and your fantasies."

He sauntered over to where she stood. Taking the beer bottle out of her hands and placing it on a rock beside his, he slowly put his arms around her waist and waited to see if she would be a participant in his plans.

"Oh, please, indulge me. I've wondered how your lips would taste under the light of the moon, and I intend to find out." He lowered his mouth to hers slowly, not wanting to take that which she didn't wish to give over willingly. He swelled when she offered no resistance, instead, becoming an accomplice.

Exploring her lips, he lost track of time. She liked the interplay of their tongues, spent long seconds licking his and letting him do the same. He became lost in her taste and the sensations she created.

At first, it was a gentle expression of attraction between two adults who were both obviously curious. But that soon built into more. His body coiled with an aching need to know hers, be inside her, and love her. His message of gentleness didn't change, but his needs did, and the budding desire became a hungry twisting demand to make her want him too.

Invested in him as he was with her, he noted that she ignored the chances he gave her to step back. And that added fuel to the intenseness. Throaty moans suddenly rang in the still of the night as she let him know she liked how he made her feel. That's when he promised every God in the universe he'd be their boy if she just didn't end the beautiful start of lovemaking before it went further.

She didn't.

In fact, she pushed herself into him, grinding her chest into his, her hips slipping into perfect position to give him the delightful knowledge of her willingness.

Ravenous and rigid, he forced himself to take things one move at a time, not to rush her or go further than her inclinations allowed. Taut, throbbing, he gently pushed her jacket aside and moved his hands to her breasts, a frontal attack to let her know his intentions and give her a chance to stop him

Only she didn't. While licking his neck and around his ears, she purred her contentment. Then she drove an electric shock through his system with her whispered words, "You really think this is the best place for this to happen, boy-o?"

He held her away from him and smiled into her shining, sultry eyes. "It's perfect. What do you think?"

"What more could a girl want? An ocean lit by moonlight, soft breezes, and we even have a blanket in the saddlebag on the back of the bike."

"Then don't go away. I'll be right back." Feeling like a lusting teenager, Sam fetched the blanket and moved them behind some bushes that would shield them from any passing motorist. He spread it out and then waited for her to join him there. Lowering next to him, she wrapped her arms around her knees and sat silent, sipping her beer while surveying the gorgeous view.

"Tell me more about Sam Reagan. What matters to you?"

Realizing that not all foreplay involved touching, he settled beside her and answered, "Let me think. I have only one close family member living so I guess you would say my sister and her children hold the position of importance at the top of the Reagan tree. Then comes the people who I work with, especially the ones here in Rhodes, who I tend to depend on more than any others." He glanced at her and sipped at his bottle. "What about you?"

"Oh, I'm fortunate to have a large family of two sisters and three brothers. I'm the eldest. The first few years of my life were lived in Canada where I was born."

Interested, Sam questioned, "Where abouts in Canada?"

"On the east coast, St. John's, Newfoundland. My mother was Greek and so I spent every summer here in Rhodes with my grandmother until I went to college and then on to training at Quantico. My mother passed a few years ago, and I swear that's one of the reasons for Yaya's quick downhill slide. She loved my mother fiercely."

"As she did you."

Sophia turned his way and nodded. "You could say that. We were always close, but when Mom died, Yaya became more... ahh, I guess needy's the word. I hated not being able to see her more than a few times a year. She would have come to Washington if she could have traveled, but the last year was difficult for her... a woman who'd always been so active. It was she who taught me to ride."

"I figured as much. I saw her photos in the living room of you and her on your bikes, riding together. And the prizes you both won. She was a beautiful woman."

"Yes. She lived a very full life until the sickness struck. The city still bemoans her loss because of the activities she invested so much of her time and energy in... homelessness, hunger, the church."

Sensing her sadness, Sam changed the subject. "What about your father and the rest of your family?"

This brought an instant smile. "I guess you could say he's the reason I'm an agent. He's a decorated cop and did a lot of good during his time on the force. But when Mom passed, he decided to move back home to St. John's where most of my brothers and sisters live, and he spends his days on his boat fishing."

"Why do I get the feeling that you're probably a good sailor too?"

"Must be because my younger years were spent in Newfoundland alongside him whenever he took out the Silver." She saw his head turn questioningly and added, "Silver Joy was the name he gave his boat because of my mom's hair. And he always referred to her as his joy. He loved her until the end, and to this day remains faithful. We all tried telling him he was young and deserved to find love again, but he's stubborn, doesn't see it that way. Says he's happy on the Joy and to quit pestering him. He comes to Washington every few months to catch up with Bill and check up on me. You'd like him. He's a man's man."

"No doubt, we'd get along. We both like silver-haired beauties." Sam sat in thought for a few seconds and then continued, "If they're back in Canada, how did you make the move to Washington?"

"Oh, right. I guess it is kind of complicated if you don't know the story. My dad's best friend moved to Washington with his family and became an FBI agent. There was a huge case many years ago, a serial killer who started out in Canada and eventually took himself off to do his dirty deeds in the U.S., ending up in Washington. My dad was lead on the case and became totally invested in catching this killer. The prick had over twenty murders under his belt and Dad and Bill colluded to get the guy. In order to work the case together, Bill sponsored our family into moving there and helped Dad get hired by the Washington police department. All of us lived in D.C. for about five years until Mom got sick. She missed our old house so badly, they'd never sold it, and so the rest of them moved back to the Rock. I stayed because I'd started my training by then and had a future with the FBI. Bill promised he'd take me under his wing, and so Dad agreed. And here we are. All scattered, but I'd be tellin' you, we're close and homecomings are a huge party."

When Sophia put the empty bottle on the ground behind them, Sam slipped his hand into hers and held on. He chuckled. "You appear so independent; it surprises me to know you have a large family. I'm glad. When you talk about them, you seem different."

First, she glanced at their entwined hands and then into his face. "Different? Different how?"

"Oh, I don't know. Happy, I guess. Alive. Hell, I can't put it in words. You're just softer."

"You sayin' I'm usually a hard ass?"

He grinned, "What I'm sayin' is, you *could* be a real hard-ass if you put your mind to it."

Teasing, and shocking the hell out of him, she pushed him down and leaned over him. "Listen, Sam-my-man, I'm a real pussycat, and don't you forget it." Her lips found his, and her kiss was soft and sweet and way too brief.

Chapter Thirty-five

Sophia had never known a man's mouth to be so perfect. His lips had a way of welcoming her tongue, and she could spend hours just tasting his unique flavor. She'd never found herself in such a predicament before. To her, lovemaking had been a friendly kind of sharing. Two people who liked each other, experiencing sexual relief and some fun together.

For her, it was never serious and if she sensed her partners becoming too involved, she'd back off damn quick. Until she finally met the one guy she couldn't give up, she behaved the way most bachelor-loving males would. Only, before any man had a chance to pull that shit on her, she did so first.

Love 'em and wave goodbye had been her motto from the beginning of her having any sexual life, and she liked things that way. Her in charge – never allowing her feelings to be involved, and an easy exit when the time came.

Only tonight, her body was betraying her. With sensations building inside she'd never felt before, she wasn't in charge. And it scared the sass right out of her.

Scrambling away from him, she couldn't believe that he'd stop her with one word, achingly said, "*stay.*"

She hesitated and turned back to his waiting lips. His fingers threaded through her hair, holding her face so he could take control. This time when they kissed, his body rolled over the top of hers and his weight held her under him.

His lips, dangerous as hell with such passion she had a hard time breathing, he let her know that he was totally invested. He needed her, and she'd better make up her mind they would be doing this his way... or not at all.

This time, his kiss, serious as pain, took her out of herself, and she flew into a place of sensations and passion... and need. Shudders and thrills, torment, and.... surrender.

Hands, warm yet knowing, slipped under her shirt, lifted her bra, and cupped her breasts. Caressing yet gentle, they made the swelling mounds ache and the sweet link of desire travel to where dampness pooled and mind-blowing pulsations began.

She'd known lust before and liked it. But this

was different, hard grains of sugar to a warm thick coating of sweet honey different. If she continued, she knew this time she'd be losing control. Best make up her mind. Could she hand over the reins?

To Sam?

Now?

Was there really any choice?

Once his hands had taught her body how delightful they could make her feel, the joy they could bring, she didn't have a hope in hell of pushing him away and giving up those delights.

Instead, she let him do what he wished. And he wished her to be naked as much as she wanted the same. It was only a matter of a few minutes before they both had taken off their clothes and were savoring each other's bodies. She loved smoothing his back, caressing the muscles that played there as he moved in on her, his leg over hers.

Invested in the way his hands found every spot on her skin that craved attention, she liked that his mouth followed. He had a teasing way of licking and biting that drove her insane. Her breath came in gasps, panting.

Rigid with need, his hardness nudged her soaked passage, signaling the man was ready, but she held him in her hand to be sure. While she took her time to inspect every inch, he groaned his approval and whispered a plea, "Yes, Sophia, baby. You're so sweet, so... so sweet." As she always did when this moment came, she turned away, raised her body, and urged him to enter.

Only, he didn't, and that had never happened before. Most men were glad to take what she offered. And it was never her face, her lips or even more important, her eyes for their scrutiny. Not during this part of the act. This form of screwing had always been the only way she'd accept a man. And none had ever turned her down.

Therefore, when Sam quickly turned her around to face him and then used his body to imprison hers, she didn't react. Not right away. It took seconds before she pushed at his chest, not with any force, but a resistance that came instinctively.

It was his words that stopped her reaction. "Oh no, not like that, Sophia. I need to look into your eyes when I take you. Together we do this, together or not at all." His fierce gaze made her see his seriousness and his thrilling tone made her understand he was taking charge. The first man to ever do so.

Bursting with sensations, thrilled by his macho actions, she stopped pushing him away and swiftly gathered him to her instead. Her arms lifted around his neck, and her lips rose to his. Eyes caught by his aroused scrutiny, ecstasy within reach, she gasped with delight when he entered her.

Mesmerized by his intense gaze, captured and loving it, she rose to heights of passion she never knew she could attain. Then his control snapped and suddenly his smooth, loving surges became swift, hard thrusts. Her legs lifted to surround him as she opened completely.

Melded, locked together, they devoured each other until both reached the pinnacle. Arms tight, lips joined, and names achingly called, drained and at the peak of sensations, they shot to the moon shining above as their release soared.

She quivered uncontrollably while he shuddered, which kept them locked in each other's arms for long, sweet moments.

Then he put his hands on each side of her face, gently pushing the damp hair away before he kissed each eye and whispered, "Thank you, sweetie."

Suddenly shy, feeling like she'd given away a section of her soul, she put her forehead against his chin and replied, "You're welcome."

He pulled her into his arms and held her tight against him, rocking her like one would a precious child. And she'd never felt so loved in her life. Oh my God, he'd broken through her barriers, and now she'd have to keep him.

And how was he going to feel about that?

They didn't have any time to discuss any of her thoughts because his phone rang. They stiffened. He reached to see who called, and when a number appeared, he answered. Stasia's voice screamed loud enough for Sophia to hear her too.

"They found the house. I'm hiding, but there are two men outside. And they're the same guys who attacked Sophia at the beach."

Chapter
Thirty-six

Watching a video on Sam's iPad, nestled in the big chair in the living room, Stasia decided to get up and brew herself a cup of hot chocolate. That's when she'd seen movement in the bushes in the front of the house.

Not too concerned, knowing that some of the neighbors often sat out at night and took their dogs for walks, she paused by the open curtains and watched from her hidden place. When the first man came in sight, a streak of terror shot through her body and she dropped to the floor.

Lying there quivering, tears dripping, her throat so tight that even if she wished to scream, nothing could be forced through the blockage, she tried to think. Shaking so hard, she peed out just a little of her fear before she clenched her muscles and felt the shame. Looking everywhere around her made her thoughts fly to Sophia.

How would she act?

She wouldn't be acting like big baby!

And what was it her savior had said she should do if something like this happened?

Think!

Quick!

One, one, four, seven. It flooded back, and that's when she knew next move. Hide in the closet with the combination lock on door, the one in Yaya's bedroom. Call Sophia and Sam. They would come. Her friends would save her. She mustn't let monsters find her first.

She couldn't go back to bad place. She'd die if freaks rent out her body again like God gave them right to make her toy to sell. And let sickos play with her, not care how they hurt, how she feel while they have... fun. How it made her die little bit each time they use her and leave her screaming inside with her shame.

She'd start to heal – her spirit and body. Sophia and Sam give her back her will to live. Made her want father and family. They'd promise to keep her safe and take her home. She'd believe them. The noise of the door opening came like blow from fist. She ran. They can't help her if they don't know her danger.

Crawling, slithering to Yaya's room, she locked herself in closet. Grabbing the phone Sophia once pointed to, she made her call. Shaking, she waited, cried, prayed for help before the mean bastards decide to search this bedroom.

Chapter Thirty-seven

Sophia dressed quickly and was ready before Sam. She'd reached the bike first, climbed on, and her decision brooked no argument. "I know every inch of this city. I'll get us there a hell of a lot faster than you can. Get on or stay here."

He didn't answer, just gestured her to move forward then sat behind her and held on. Pleased she didn't have to argue, she headed for the hills behind the city and took a path she and her grandmother had used many times. The only difference was that they'd never done so in the dark.

Instinct kept her on the uneven trail and led her to the steep hill, the exact spot where she'd have to turn off to get onto a road that would take them into the city, then on the back streets that led them to Yaya's house. It had only taken them a short time to get there, but to Sophia, who'd died a thousand times on the way, it seemed like too long.

Fucking bastards! She prayed the kid was smart enough to go in the closet. She'd shown her the combination lock her grandmother had installed to protect the safe she kept there, and because it gave her a place to hide if someone broke in. It could be locked both from the outside and the inside with only four digits. If only Stasia had memorized those easy numbers like she'd told her to, she'd be okay.

That's if they didn't have a gun they might use on the locking device to get to her.

Upon arrival, they left the bike at the end of the road near a neighbor's hedge and crept closer to the house. In front, further down the street sat a black SUV, the same one her and Stasia had evaded the night they'd met at the beach.

Reaching into her zipped pocket, she pulled out her own weapon she kept there for times when she rode alone at night. A girl could never be too careful no matter where she lived. It had become her custom to never leave home without a weapon.

Her grin appeared when Sam reached down to his ankle holster and retrieved his own Glock 33. How he'd managed to keep that from her, she didn't know or care. Right now, she just felt thankful he would be her backup.

She slipped into the neighbor's yard, calling to the growling dog to pat him quiet, and urged Sam to follow. At the back of the garden a gate sat hidden by a huge bougainvillea plant filled with bright pink blossoms. Careful to stay low, she easily leapt the barrier and motioned for him to do so too. She knew the squeaking gate could alert someone in her house who would be listening for any strange noises.

Keeping her gun close to her chest, she first made sure no guard was there. Whispering to him that he needed to let her go before him and getting his nod of agreement, she ran to a basement window, undid the latch, and held it open so he could be the first to enter the house.

Then she tumbled into the darkness, his hands catching her to break her hard landing. Both listened to whatever noises they could hear and when the gunshot rang out, both jumped and then ran toward the sound, Sophia first.

She hit the stairs two at a time, Sam close behind. When she opened the door leading to the hallway that took them to the bedrooms, she crouched low and scanned everywhere, her gun in both hands. Listening, praying no other shots would follow, she made her way to the bedroom where she'd advised Stasia to hide.

Coming closer, they heard the commotion, the screams, then the begging. When Sophia appeared in the doorway, she let them know she wasn't playing games. Her voice as cold as a black witch's glare gave the command, "Let her go. Now!"

Stasia had blood on her hands from clinging to

the shot-up, broken doorframe, fighting hard to stop them from dragging her away. Sophia had arrived just as the bigger arse had his fist ready to drive it into the girl's stomach, probably warned not to mark the merchandise by hitting her in the face.

Sam hadn't appeared, and she wondered at his reasons for hanging back. Not letting it stop her, she shot the gun from the hand of the arsehole who was stupid enough to aim it her way, then she quickly whipped her weapon toward the other creep intending on getting to her. "Stay back, boy-o, or I'll shoot you, and nobody could say I didn't have just cause."

"You stole our property. We just came to collect."

"G'wan with ya. She's a girl, she's no one's property, and I didn't steal her. In case you didn't notice the other night, she came willingly. Looks to me like right now, she's fighting to stay here too."

"Yeah? Well, she's coming back because she knows we have her family covered. If she doesn't, we can go to her pa and tell him she's broken her commitment to us. If there's a scene, he could be hurt. You know what I'm saying? Maybe it's best if you get out of our way. Let us leave with the bitch and there's no more trouble."

His words rang with conviction. She saw Stasia flinch and then drop to the ground in terror. "No, not my papa. Please. Don't do this. I can't go back.

I better to die."

Knowing she couldn't go to the girl, Sophia still let her attention sway for the few seconds it took the empty-handed pissant to rush her, only to meet up with Sam's fist seemingly coming out of thin air. He still hadn't fully appeared, keeping his back to the room.

But the knowledge there was another made it plain that they didn't have the upper hand. The talker pushed the girl toward Sophia to block his getaway. As he passed the two in combat, he drove his fist into Sam's back to make him loosen his grip on his buddy, and then he ran for the door.

The other scrambled to his feet, fighting hard to get away, and Sophia had no doubt Sam allowed him to do so. That didn't make any sense and neither did the fact that he hadn't stuck with her from the beginning. He'd let her enter the fight alone. She needed answers and from the closed expression of his face, he didn't appear to be in a talking mood.

Chapter
Thirty-eight

Stasia rushed to Sophia. Close to passing out from fear, she clung and sobbed her relief at having been saved.

"Don't cry, honey. You're okay. No need to be scared. We're here." Sophia looked at Sam. "We have to leave the house." Sophia made the decision but Sam nodded in agreement. After she calmed Stasia down, cleaned and bandaged her hands, they packed up their gear.

She called Barney to book two rooms. Driving her grandmother's car, they were on the road within an hour. All during that time, Sophia calmed Stasia, telling her she did the right thing, and she was proud of her quick thinking.

Exhausted by the stress from earlier, Stasia eventually put on the earphones to listen to her music. She settled in the backseat in the corner, rested her head against the window and soon fell asleep.

That's when Sophia shot Sam a hard look and asked, "What happened to you back at the house?"

He glanced her way, shock lighting his features. "What do you mean?"

"I mean, you hung back."

"I was there. I stepped in when you needed me and—"

Interrupting his excuses, she snarled, "You let me go in alone." Sophia hated that her tone held the hurt she'd tried to hide.

"Sweetie, you were safe every moment. I had my gun pointed at both those assholes through the opening of the door frame. Look, the big guy knew me, we met once in the States, and he would have blown my cover, told Manos I was here. Those kids would have disappeared, and we'd be up shit creek. I couldn't take the chance."

Mollified, in fact, totally understanding the choice he'd had to make and remembering he'd stepped in when she'd needed him, she reached her hand across and lowered her voice.

"I'm sorry. I should have known you'd never leave me. That you'd have had a good reason for acting that way. It's just I've never been able to depend on a partner in the past. Personality conflicts got in the way both times I tried and then I took special training so I could work alone."

"I know. I read your files. Man, you really can shoot. That was a fine hit, knocking the gun from that prick's hand and not shooting off any fingers."

"I would have but didn't see any reason to piss him off to where it got personal. A man with a grudge like that is dangerous and right now, we don't need any vindictive bullshit getting in the way of us closing them down."

"Which is exactly why I hung back like I did. But I'll tell you something, Sophia."

"What's that?"

"I never want to go through another moment like that again. It was fucking excruciating."

She heard his message, the fear he let her see from the way he spoke the last word, and it became clear. He'd suffered. Which meant he cared for her.

Good!

Because when she thought he'd left her alone to face the danger, cracks had begun shattering her newly aroused heart, and she never wanted to live through such pain again.

***

As late as it was, Barney met them at the hotel entrance. Speaking to Sophia, he explained why. "When you booked rooms, the front desk notified me as they were supposed to do. We had a last-minute cancellation on a cottage, and I thought it might be perfect for you and your guests." He checked out Stasia first, smiled at her, and then turned to Sam with his hand extended. "Barney Adamos."

Sam shook hands and added, "Sam Reagan. I'm

an associate of Sophia's, but no one should know that I'm here." Sam watched Barney's reaction and was pleased that all he did was nod. He waited for Sam to park the car and then headed up the path to where they would be staying.

"If you need anything at all, call the front desk and Jorge will look after you. He's very discreet and will make sure no one knows about you checking in." When they arrived at the luxurious cabin, lit up to show a huge covered deck with wonderful views, the motion lights brightened as soon as they stepped within certain boundaries.

Once he unlocked the door and ushered them inside, he added, "It's fully stocked with supplies thanks to the thoughtfulness of the canceled guests. If you need anything, let me or Jorge know, and we'll see to it." He put his arm around Sophia's shoulders and added, "Can I talk with you for a minute in private."

Sam caught Barney's eye, saw they had a mutual fondness for each other, and relaxed his chauvinistic tendencies not to let her out of his sight. Safe now, he didn't have to worry about being found here. Not by the bastards who somehow knew what house in town they'd stayed in.

Had he tipped them off? Had they been trailing him? He'd taken such care not to be followed, and he was damn good at it. Had Sophia led them there? Again, she was FBI and would never let herself be spied on without her knowledge.

Then how the hell had they found Stasia?

While Sophia was on the deck with her cousin, he went to where Stasia was making a coffee in the machine provided. "Hey kiddo, I need to know something. Did you make a call to one of your friends at the house?"

Stasia dropped the mug from her hands, and it crashed to the floor. The stark white color that flooded her face proved her guilt. "I had to call Maria. She is only eleven. I wanted her to know we come to help her soon. Sam, I was like sister for her. I know losing me will be hard, that she is sad, maybe give up... wish to die." As she spoke, she slid to her knees, begging him to understand. "I did bad thing." Her beseeching gaze had him rushing to her. "Didn't I? And they find me. I am so sorry."

Sam lifted her from the floor and sat her in a chair. He pulled another one close so he could watch her face and let her see his. "No, honey, don't apologize for caring, Stasia. It's just that we have more going on here than just freeing your friends. Those men can't find us again. We need to stay out of their way so they can't stop us from closing them down. Do you understand?"

"Yes. I'm sorry. It is my fault. I never would phone her if I know they can find me because of call."

"Chances are, they had her phone set up so if you made a call, they could intercept. There is one thing I've wondered though. Why did they give you phones? You've mentioned before that you had one, but you left it at the hotel."

"They told us it is allowed we only call them on these phones and only if we need them to pick us up... or if we have trouble. They said phones were cheap – best to have for safety. But I memorize Maria's number, and she did mine, so we can call each other sometimes."

"Why didn't you tell me. I would have taken you to a public phone where they couldn't have traced you."

"I don't know, Sam. While I was alone, the phone in house rang. I didn't answer it – like you said not too. Barney's voice says he's checking to be sure Sophia comes to dinner tomorrow. I think he wants to chat like he said in the message. I like his voice. He makes jokes. It makes me think. Maybe I call Maria. If she isn't with customer, we talk too."

"You'll be able to talk with her very soon, honey. Just hang in there and trust me and Sophia."

Stasia threw her arms around Sam's neck and hugged tight, her stress now lessened, her fears seeming to be under control. "I wish to find way I repay you and Sophia. I clean for you, wash clothes, look after house. I like to be busy. At home, I take care for my sisters and brothers, not just hang around with lazy hands and too much time."

Chapter
Thirty-nine

Once Barney had Sophia alone, he lit in. "What's going on? You wouldn't be calling for rooms in the middle of the night unless something happened. And seeing the shock on that pretty girl's face, and her bandaged hands, I'm thinking it wasn't good."

Sophia knew she could trust her cousin. He'd defend her with his life, but she had no right to expect it from him. Or to bring any kind of threat to his family or his home. "Barney, I'm ninety-nine percent sure that coming here tonight will in no way endanger you, Ellie or the hotel. Stasia and Sam just needed a place to lie low for the next few days and me being here would not seem unusual to anyone."

"Of course not. You've stayed here plenty of times. But what about the others? What's their stories?"

"Sam owns the Reagan Group based out of

Miami. Maybe you've heard of it?"

"Of course, I have. He's a bigshot in law enforcement circles, or should I say his company is. They have a stellar reputation."

"Yes. I know. He's working on a case involving human trafficking right now."

"Seriously? In Rhodes? Lordy, that shocks me."

"I know. It shocked Yanis too. Look, I can't tell you much about what's happening other than to say the girl, Stasia, is a victim. She's a sweet thing, comes from a large family in Sochi, and wanted to help her widowed father. She opted to take the job offer from men who came to her factory, conning quite a few youngsters to sign on for a better life. They convinced them to come to Greece, work hard, and be able to send money home."

"Instead they force them to what... work in brothels?"

"Yes."

"Sons a bitches! How did you find her?"

"She had the guts to run away from her jailers. I met up with her on the beach and took her under my wing."

Barney grinned at Sophia and ruffled her hair, something no one else would ever get away with. "You're everyone's warrior, cuz."

"Barney, she's been badly hurt, probably scarred forever. Right now, she needs to feel human again, and that she's worthy."

Barney nodded, his face suddenly serious.

"Well, I'll keep her busy for now working with Ellie and the kids. If she's everything you say she is, maybe we can come to an arrangement for her to stay on. How old is she?"

"I'd say fifteen at the most."

"Then she should go back to school, shouldn't she?"

"It would be the best possible conclusion. But not until next year. By then she'll have completely succeeded in learning English. And she'll have put this horrible experience behind her. Time has a way of healing open wounds."

"Yes. Like you missing Yaya. You're dealing much better now than when she first passed." He closed in on her, his hand rubbing her shoulder. "We can see what happens with Stasia. Of course, it depends on whether Ellie and the children like her. And if she likes us."

"That would be ideal, Barney. But I think you should call her Anna while she's here. Stasia isn't as common and might be recognized."

"Good idea. Best to keep her presence hidden, right?"

She grinned his way. "You keep being this nice, I might have to give you a hug."

"Seriously? Are you feeling okay?" He laughed when instead she slugged his arm.

***

Barney and Sophia happened to walk in just as Stasia made her announcement that she needed something to do. And it was Barney who spoke first. "If you really mean that, I have five kids who are driving my wife a little batty right now. Three of them have colds, aren't allowed out, and demand constant attention. If you want to help, young lady, I'd be glad to pay you for any hours you're willing to spare. If you can keep those monsters occupied, read to them, and play with them, you'll be a lifesaver. My poor Ellie is close to losing her mind about now and would bless you."

Sophia looked toward Sam to confirm approval, and he nodded back. Then he spoke to Stasia. "Would you like to help Barney out? If so, you know you must stay away from the other guests and not let anyone see you."

Barney turned to Sophia and cut in, "In case you're worried about the Russian guests we had here earlier, I've asked them to leave, and they departed this morning. They were rowdy and rude. The rest of our vacationers are a fun bunch. So, she should be safe from prying eyes. But we do have back doors to our private home. I'll show her so she never has to be in the main lobby or any of the guest areas."

Sam made the final decision. "Then I think it's an ideal solution to keep her occupied while giving us the freedom to do what needs to be done. Things will be coming to a head very soon, and there's a lot of planning and organizing before we make any moves. What do you think, Sophia?"

"If Stasia would like to do this, then I agree." She turned to see a delighted girl, her hands clasped in front like in prayer. "Stasia? Are you okay with this arrangement?"

"Yes, please."

"Then it's settled."

Barney's expression had lit with interest when he'd heard Sam speak about the operation getting exciting soon. His last words didn't surprise. "Sam count me in if you need something I can provide."

Sam wished that were possible, but before he could ask any favors from Barney, he needed to make a call.

Chapter
Forty

While Sophia and Stasia got themselves organized with rooms, showers, and a midnight snack, Sam went to the deck where warm breezes blew away the earlier tensions, and he found himself relaxing.

He'd seen the security system the cabin provided. Brand new sensors, small cameras located in different locations, and all kinds of up-to-date technology to keep them safe and intruders outside.

He relaxed on a lounger and made his call to David. "Did you watch the car while we drove toward Lindos? Anyone following us?"

"Of course, I watched. Weren't those your orders? Boss, you got away clean. Whoever those bastards were, they didn't tail you, I guarantee it."

"Thanks, bud. I can sleep a bit easier now. Did the rest of the gang touch base? From Athens and the other islands?"

"I'm still waiting to hear they're set up in Mykonos, but the others are ready to move in whenever we give the word. Oh, and Sam, that ship in the U.S. will be arriving in three days, early evening. Only thing left to do is figure out which container out of how many hundreds is carrying the goods."

"And I've no doubt between you and John-john working on the puzzle, you'll have it settled by the time they arrive in harbor."

His voice changing, filled with worry now, David's answer didn't relieve his concern. "I bloody well hope so. We're miracle workers, but not Gods."

***

The next morning and early afternoon, Sophia took Ellie for a break to Lindos and ate lunch at their favorite restaurant on the beach while Barney supervised Stasia with the children – his way of making sure she was suitable. Totally understandable to Sophia's way of thinking. And she had no doubt he'd fall under the girl's spell as her and Sam had done.

Bearing gifts for the kids, Sophia arrived a few hours later for the promised dinner and was greeted by her nieces and nephew. They were full of excitement about their new caregiver, who they called Anna, and sang her praises so much that she breathed a sigh of relief for having solved one problem.

Glad they'd decided that Anastasia should use that nickname while at the hotel, it would throw any interested party off the track if the kids or even Ellie or Barney slipped up and talked about their newest employee. With Manos coming that evening, they needed to play it safe.

She did ask Ellie, Barney, and Yanis a favor after she arrived. "Please don't mention anything about my FBI position to anyone."

"Because of Manos?"

"Why do you say that?"

"Because you brought up everyone else except him."

Thinking quickly, she said, "That's because he doesn't know I work for the Bureau. At the barbecue, he said you'd told him I work for the government in Washington. That could mean a number of different positions. I'm glad now that there's so few of us that I won't have to worry it might slip out."

"Can you tell me why we need to keep quiet about something you know I like to brag about?"

"Not really. All I can say is that it's an ongoing case here in Rhodes that with luck will be settled by the end of the week."

When she looked around, Barney lifted his finger to his mouth as a way of saying she needn't worry about what he knew. He'd kept it to himself. Good!

She'd seen the wink Yanis had given her before

he'd wrapped her in a bear hug and whispered, "I've gotten the others on board with what's going on, Sophia. We'll be ready when you give the word about stepping in."

She whispered back, "It won't be much longer. Make sure they're willing to shut down the mayor and his lackey, the police commander."

"Go figure, that dipshit is on the wrong side. He's got a handful of officers that answer only to him, and we know exactly who they are. We'll be ready."

"Don't mention anything tonight."

"Got it. How is the girl, Stasia?"

"We're calling her Anna here, and she's fine."

The ringing of the outer bell announced the arrival of the last guest and Manos appeared. A sense of excitement bristled around the well-dressed man. He emitted an aura of eagerness that seemed to stem from his meeting again with Sophia.

She'd chosen a shell-pink dress of filmy material that floated around her ankles as she walked. Her tan showed off well in the outfit as did her slim figure and silver hair. She knew she looked okay, but from the raving enthusiasm Manos showered on her, uneasiness struck from the moment of his arrival.

Obviously smitten, the man followed her around like a puppy and constantly gave compliments that might have delighted some women but just made her feel rather ill. Every time she looked his way, she imagined duct tape across his deceitful mouth so his lush lips couldn't flap.

"You look ravishing, Sophia. I looked forward to meeting you again so much that tonight couldn't come soon enough."

Speaking truthfully, Sophia replied with a grin. "Funny you say that. I feel the same way. And I'm looking forward to visiting your home tomorrow. Barney tells me you've been doing some redecorating."

"Yes, the old place needed a total redo. I've replaced the livestock, built a stable, bought new horses, and even put in a pool. My investments have earned me enough recently that I wanted to make sure my children have a comfortable and safe home in Rodos."

"Spoken like a thoughtful parent. Your twins are much younger than your eldest boy."

"Yes, their mother is an American. Alex's mama is a girl I met years ago in Athens. Right now, she's on a modeling shoot in Europe and has left the boy with me for a time. But... it seems he likes his life with his father, and so I'm thinking we should come to a new arrangement for his future."

Buttering up his oversized ego, she spoke softly, "I imagine any boy would be thrilled to hang out with you and learn about life on a ranch."

Pleased and showing it, he took the bait and admitted his younger boy didn't see things that way at all. "As I told you at the barbecue, my twins aren't settling down as I'd hoped. Casey cries a lot. Jack did too until I taught him that boys don't behave that way. Now he's toughening up. It's good."

Hearing these words, Sophia knew when the time came, she'd take great joy in putting this dipshit away for a lot of years. Scum like him, a man who pretended to care for his kids when all he cared about was sticking it to his ex-wife, a man who could be the reason so many immigrants were being abused, their rights destroyed by his greed, didn't deserve her consideration.

"You know, Manos. I've promised my nephew, Barney's boy Peter, a trip across to Marmaris in Turkey for a special treat." She pulled the fake poster Sam had given her from her purse and showed him the colorful page. "There'll be pony rides, and all kinds of games and fun treats for the kids. I understand they have special merry-go-round rides and clowns and a petting zoo. I can't bring Barney's girls because they have a birthday party they're invited to, and when Peter found out he wasn't allowed to go to an all-girl sleepover, he threw a fit. The only way we could appease his hurt feelings was for me to promise him a boat ride on one of the tourist Catamarans and a day at this park. Do you think your twins might like to come with me?"

Manos took some time studying the poster and

said, "This is the day after tomorrow. I'm committed to meetings all day."

"Oh, well. I could take them myself if you wouldn't mind. Three kids I can handle, and your two seem like good children."

Barney, listening in on the conversation, had been warned what she needed him to say. He leaned over as if he just overheard their topic and added, "Sophia saved us from a full day of pouting by offering to take Peter on this delightful trip. It's all he's been talking about since she told him yesterday."

Manos looked at Barney and Ellie, both who smiled their pleasure and slowly nodded, "I think the children would be more than happy to have a day with you, Sophia."

Concerned that he meant to include Alex, she stepped in first. "I'm not sure Alexandro would be happy with the little ones, being forced to go on baby rides. He's such a little man, he might feel it beneath him. What do you think?"

"You're right. He likes to hang out at the stables and spends most of his day with the men, riding, and fencing. He'd hate to be forced to go on this type of excursion. Plus, the twins would enjoy their day much more if he didn't go."

Sophia could see that the man knew of the rivalry between his children and his redeeming feature, showing that he cared, gave her the ability to carry on the rest of the evening. Not that every time she looked at his chauvinistic actions, she didn't want to physically hurt him.

But for now, she'd play the game because she knew, in the end, he'd pay. And the satisfaction of knowing she'd be one of the players in making it happen gave her the strength to continue in her role.

Dinner passed painfully slow. If the others hadn't been with them, Yanis, who relieved her as often as politeness made it possible, and Barney and Ellie, who tried to break into the conversation and steer it to them all having a full-table discussion rather than Manos hoarding all her attention, Sophia would have been forced to fake a headache and escape.

When his phone rang, and the anger from the one-sided conversation reddened his face and had him irritably forcing the cell back into his pocket, she knew something was up. Worry assailed until he admitted what happened. "My Russian friends were gambling and drinking excessively. They started a brawl and the local police stepped in and want to press charges. I need to leave and try to help."

Barney asked, "Those must be the same Russians I asked to leave my hotel yesterday. They're party animals."

"Yes. I'm glad you did so. They're trouble and need to go home. I'll be explaining that just as soon as I get this mess cleared up." Manos's tone turned ugly, his disgust apparent. "Crazy fools." He glanced around at the others and let his gaze fall on Sophia last. "I hate to leave this way. I've had such a good time." He took her hand before she knew he would, and she let him hold it, knowing he'd be gone soon. "I'm so sorry about this, Sophia. I had hoped we could spend more time tonight getting to know each other. I'm glad we have tomorrow to look forward to."

"I'm sorry this came up too, Manos. But I do understand that friends must come first. I'll see you tomorrow."

As he waved his last goodbye before following Ellie to the door, she wondered how she going to get through the next night without committing murder. As painful as the idea was, it had to be done. She'd laid the beginning of her plan out and no way did she want to do anything to stop it from happening.

She was so close.

Chapter
Forty-one

After Yanis and Manos were both gone, Sophia called Sam to join in on a final nightcap with Ellie and Barney.

Watching the tall man enter through the back door, she felt satisfaction surge. The man was the total opposite of the son of a bitch she'd spent the evening with so that when his gaze found hers immediately, and he winked a special hello, goosebumps broke out all over.

A weird kind of shyness attacked, a lovely feeling of importance. She'd never been so attracted to anyone before, and it left her feeling vulnerable. She noticed Barney's stare, followed by his stupid grin, and quickly put up her shield before Sam himself saw her weakness.

The man had enough self-assurance, he certainly didn't need for her to let him see how infatuated she was.

Sam accepted a beer from Barney, and they settled into a discussion on how much Ellie and Barney had appreciated having Stasia helping in their household that day.

"She's a gem, Sam. So gentle with the girls and treats Peter like the little man he should be. I never want her to leave." Ellie's tone said it all. She meant every word, and both Sam and Sophia were thrilled that Stasia was safe and happy. They'd listened to her earlier raving about how wonderful the Adamos family were, how nicely they treated their children and her as well, and so it seemed like a mutually satisfying situation.

They discussed the plan for Sophia to take Manos's kids to Turkey and reiterated their agreement that Peter could go along. Since they'd planned a trip to Virginia to visit with Ellie's parents that next week anyway, they offered to pick Peter up in Washington where Sophia would keep him with her until they arrived.

Sophia had worried whether Manos would allow her to take his twins to Turkey alone, and so she'd called Barney and Ellie to ask if she might invite their Peter to go along with them. She'd hoped it would validate the trip and make Manos less anxious for her to take the twins.

What Manos didn't know was the actual fair with the clowns and the rides were in Washington and that David had just changed the dates and place on the fake poster.

As parents do, they knew Peter would be thrilled to have a holiday with his favorite cousin. And though the girls were jealous, knowing they would also be seeing Sophia in Washington helped put an end to their envy.

Walking back to the cottage, Sam reached for her hand and never knew the difficult decision she made to allow him the privilege. It wasn't something she'd ever let another boyfriend do. She didn't like to feel tethered to a man, and though she knew it was dumb, it never mattered enough for her to change her mind... until tonight.

While they strolled along the empty beach, moonlight filtered through the few clouds meandering across the sky. She leaned her head on his shoulder and let all the stress from the last few days ease.

Being here with him like this was heaven. Having his undivided attention, a huge boon to her hidden insecurities. All her sisters and brothers had settled with their partners years earlier and were leading happy married lives that she envied. For her, giving over control to a man wouldn't come easy.

His voice broke into her thoughts and she began to listen to his words. It almost seemed he'd read her mind. "I've never met a woman who made me feel like I was... home." He stopped walking, turned to her, and put his hands on her arms. "You're slipping so deep inside me; I can barely keep my mind on the job. And that's never happened to me before. I'm not sure how to handle it. So, if I screw up, don't freak out on me. This is all so new."

"Me? Freak out?" she chuckled without any real humor attached to the noise. "Why would you say that? I'm as defenseless with this... this happening to us as you are. You think I've ever met someone like you before? Let myself become involved to this extent?"

"That's just it, I don't know. Have you?"

"Would you believe me if I said I've never let anyone close in on me like you have. And in just a few days. It scares the hell out of me so much that I don't like it. Feeling this... this vulnerable."

He leaned in and kissed her very gently, and then stood back so he could look into her eyes. "Then you do understand."

She allowed him to delve into her gaze until she felt like she would drown if he looked a moment longer. That's when she put her forehead on his chest. And that's when he lifted his hand to caress her hair and place a kiss there. His voice mesmerized. "We'll take it slow."

"Just don't stop."

"Oh, that'll never happen. Not now that I've found you. You're stuck with me as your shadow forever."

"That's a long time."

"Not long enough. I haven't even begun to learn everything there is to know about you."

"If you want to know the truth, I'm rather boring. I work, watch a little TV, read a lot, cook when I have to and exercise every day. See... boring."

He laughed. "Then I must be boring as well because you've just listed my routine when I'm not on a job. And you know what, I like my life."

"Me too. It took me a while before I realized I didn't need parties and entertainment all the time like some of the girls at work. When home, I do what I want and enjoy the peace. I have a cozy little condo in D.C. with a rooftop garden and neighbors who are willing to look after things when I'm gone. What about you?"

"I finally bought a small house in Miami. It's a place to hang my hat for the few times I'm stateside. I'm not attached, it's just somewhere to head to when the job is done and another hasn't started yet. Our headquarters are there so it seemed to be where I needed a home."

He put his arm around her shoulders and began walking toward a picturesque bench closer to the waves. There he brushed off the sand before he'd let her take a seat and settled himself next to her. "Truth is, the Reagan Group is becoming overloaded. There's so much work out in the world, I should be a fulltime boss rather than overseeing assignments myself."

"That I can believe. It's like the wild west in so many places today."

"So, you get it. I've always told myself that when the time came, if we needed to expand, it would be me at the helm. That I wouldn't let anyone else run my firm or organize it in ways that aren't mine."

"I can see that. It's your baby. I don't blame you. The world's a small place today, but that doesn't mean there aren't universal laws we should all live by. There's so much corruption potential that without some controls, we could lose our humanity. Kind of like what's happening here in Rhodes at the house where they held Stasia."

"That's right. It's why I started my business in the first place. In the military, we were always restricted by tradition and the stages of command. By the time we could get to the top brass for permission to go ahead, most of the time it would be too late. I decided there were too many instances where a small covert team of top military-styled veterans could really make a difference. That's how we started. Marc was my first recruit and then the others followed. Soon, I had so many people wanting work and willing to be placed anywhere they were needed, that the jobs came pouring in. Now, I see we've grown too fast. I need to back us the hell off and regroup. But I never seem to get the time."

"Stop the whirlwind and make the time."

He took her face in his hands and looked deep into her eyes. "Now I have a reason to make it happen. Nothing has ever been a strong enough incentive to keep me in one place... until now." His lips found hers willing and ready. They kissed for a long time until the sighs became pants and desire became an ache filled with need.

They made their way to the cottage and entered through the side door that led directly into Sophia's room. There he took his time to undress her while kissing every inch of skin he revealed. She stood there, allowing him the freedom of her body, knowing no other had ever had her at such a disadvantage. She never did believe there was a feminine role to play to a man's masculinity... until now.

She'd taken from earlier partners as much as she allowed them to take. But, Sam was different. Her body knew him, thrilled for him... burned for him. And there lay the difference.

His hands traveled everywhere they wanted until she finally realized he was as much hers for the taking as the other way around. That's when she stumbled on the fact that he liked to be petted and stroked. Her mouth on him drove him insane, and her power over the warrior knew no bounds. Like putty in her hands, he allowed her to see the sway she held. And so, she gave back the same.

Lying together on the silky sheets, he entered her and there was no hesitation, only desire so strong that their bodies reached a pinnacle neither had ever experienced.

That's when he called her name, achingly,

sweetly, filled with such tenderness that it brought tears to her eyes. Her answer came softly.

"I'm here, my Sam. I'm here."

Chapter
Forty-two

The next morning, after Stasia disappeared next door, Sam decided to check in with Marc and the others at the house on Kennenti while Sophia opted to go to her Yaya's house and start packing it up so when she left, everything would be ready.

"Should you be going there alone, Sophia? They know about the place. Sure you don't want me with you?"

Bristling slightly, she put her hands on her hips, fell back on words her Dad used, and glared. "So soon? I knows you're not stunned. You want to start that shit, already?"

Laughing at her back-home speech, he held up both hands and stepped back. "No! God, no, my little pumpkin. I'm good. Just being sure you have everything you need."

"Just so you know, boy-o, I can take care of myself. Don't you ever think I can't."

Sam knew she kidded, but there was just enough seriousness behind the joking that he got it and said so. "And that's why I feel secure in knowing you'll be just fine and won't be needing my manly strength to protect you." He flexed his muscles jokingly and headed for the door when she threw the pillow she picked up at his face.

Renting a car from a close-by dealer, he headed into town and drove to the house where his people were staying. As soon as he arrived, the others began filling him in on all the operations they'd set in place for the next day. It was a lot of organizing, getting all his people settled in along with the local authorities so they'd hit every one of the stakeouts at once.

They couldn't take any chances that someone from one of the houses would warn the others and help them escape. That mustn't happen. Once Manos found out that the jig was up, that his people were being arrested, he'd obviously go into hiding, and they might not be able to capture him another time. Worse, he could stop Sophia from taking the twins. If the scum disappeared with them, Maureen might lose her chance of ever finding Jack and Casey again. Sam couldn't let that happen, not to his only family.

Suddenly, David appeared and his face let Sam know they had a problem. "What's up, guy?"

"They've moved houses."

"What? Where?"

"Here in Rhodes."

"How? What happened?"

"They've stopped going to the place we've been watching."

"What do you mean?"

"I mean, they took the hostages last evening like they always do, but they haven't returned with them. One of the black vans came back early this morning, and I just took for granted it was filled with the people, but it's not so. There's no movement around the place. Usually, the girls sit in the courtyard and have coffee by this time... not today. There's no one around. It's empty, except for the guard they left there."

Sam felt like a bomb just detonated in his chest. Sweet baby Jesus, they couldn't lose them now. Not now when they only had one day to get this right.

His gut tightened and he clenched his fists angrily. He stalked to the opposite side of the room and stopped, one hand at the back of his head and the other in his pocket, the same way he always stood when his brain kicked into top gear.

David waited, saying nothing. As usually happened, Sam came back at him with orders.

"I might have a way of locating them, but I'll have to fetch Stasia. Give me a few hours. In the meantime, start looking around the area for any other places they could be. Hopefully, they won't have moved too far away."

"We need to get that address, boss."

"Yeah, yeah. Keep working, I'll be back as soon as I can."

Chapter
Forty-three

Sophia drove to the house and let herself in carefully, not expecting trouble but still not comfortable in ignoring the chance someone might be waiting. Probably a good thing she was prepared, because when she saw the mess in her Yaya's house fierce anger exploded.

Suddenly weak, she dropped into one of the only chairs standing upright, pounded her fists on her knees, and shouted a string of cuss words that gave her some relief. Bastards couldn't help themselves. Had to trash the place.

Sons of bitches had messed with everything she held dear. They must have returned after she and Sam had taken Stasia and left. Good thing she decided they'd be safer at Barney's after all. The creeps had torn the place apart looking for some hints as to where they might have taken the kid.

Oh shit! It dawned on her that her grandmother

had her Quantico graduation photograph on her night table. Jumping over the articles strewn everywhere, she pushed aside overturned tables and crunched on broken lamps to get to the room that held her secrets.

Only the broken frame still stood there. The photograph was missing. She had no doubt who they took it to... Manos. If he didn't know before that she was in any way involved in Stasia's escape, he would know now.

Crap!!

And he'd be aware that she didn't just work for the government, but that she was an FBI agent. The quiet in the house ended when her cell phone rang. She looked at the unfamiliar number and hesitated. Her finger hit the talk button and she said her hello in the way she normally did when at home in Washington. Hoping to still play him, she spoke in a businesslike manner. "Agent Dunne."

"Sophia? Is that you?"

"Oh, I'm sorry. I thought it was my boss from Washington calling about my request for an extra week's extension on my holiday. Is that you, Manos?"

"Yes. You're an FBI agent?"

"Yes. Didn't Ellie tell you? I work for the Federal Government in Washington. I'm PA to Assistant Special Agent in Charge, Bill Bruner. He calls me his glorified secretary, but since the man couldn't tie his shoes without me, I had to clear taking an extra week with him. I can't bear the thought of leaving Rhodes after what I found today."

She listened closely to his voice and heard the steely tone hidden by politeness. "Why? What happened?"

"My grandmother's house was broken into last night while I was with you at Barney's. It's been trashed. I think they were looking for a homeless girl who I found on the beach a few days ago. I helped her, even let her stay with me, but she took off last night. The ungrateful brat didn't say goodbye, kiss my ass or nothing. Just took the money from my Yaya's stash she found and disappeared. Strange girl. You know, there were people after her. In fact, two guys broke into the house and the next-door neighbor who was having a nightcap on his back porch heard the scream, ran into the house with me, and we fought them off. Guess it scared the kid."

"My goodness. You've had quite an eventful life since you arrived." Did his voice seem less curt?

"I know. And all I wanted was to come to my favorite place in the world, settle my grandmother's affairs, meet up with old friends and family, and have a holiday. I guess now that the kid's gone, I can go back to living normally again. By the way, did you call me for something important? I'm sorry I've been rambling on about my business and forgot to ask."

"No, no. I wanted to tell you how much I... ahh,

enjoyed last night, and I'm looking forward to our dinner this evening."

"Me too, Manos. That's about the only silver lining to this day so far."

"Did you need help with cleaning up the mess there. I can come if you wish."

"Manos, that is very kind of you to offer."

"I'm a kind man, Sophia. As you will learn after we spend more time together."

Gagging silently, she chuckled. "I look forward to tonight. I have nothing else to do today so I'll take my time and sort through this mess alone. I needed to clean out the house anyway. Goodbye until later. You said six, right?"

"Yes. That's a perfect time. The twins are looking forward to your visit. They've been chattering nonstop about their outing with you tomorrow. See you later."

Sophia hung up the phone and sat, replaying their conversation. Had she come across as authentic when her loathing for the creep churned in her stomach? Never having any acting ability, the undercover work she'd been involved with in the past had taxed her skills. But she'd also built a certain talent to bullshit when necessary.

Bringing her phone up to make another call, she hesitated. Should she tell Sam? Would he let her go tonight if he saw this mess? He might cancel the whole plan and take his men in to grab the kids, rather than go along with the original proposal.

She'd hoped that by telling some portion of the truth to Manos, it would relieve whatever questions arose if – or should she say when – they showed him her photograph. She'd admitted to being employed by the FBI. She also admitted to finding Stasia and trying to help her. Telling him that her neighbor helped fight off the people who broke in the other night was another diversion. She didn't want him to think she was involved with any other man. And most important, she couldn't let him think her status as an agent was any danger to him or his operation.

Did he still believe she was there to have a holiday? She'd find out in a few hours because she had every intention of following through with her original strategy. Therefore, it might be a better idea for her to keep this mess to herself. She lowered the phone.

But then she remembered a promise to a distraught mom.

"Hi, Sissy. I'm amazed at how easy it was to reach you." Sophia asked for the governor and within a few seconds had been put through.

"I made sure your number was posted at the house and here at the office. That way, if any calls came through, I would be notified at once. Have you seen Jack and Casey? Please tell me they're okay."

"They're okay. But they miss their mom. Poor little tykes have each other and it helps. I've set up a plan to get the kids out tomorrow. We'll be flying from Marmaris, Turkey. Sam, your brother, will contact you with the arrangements." She spoke with a teasing note in her voice when she mentioned Sam.

"You've met him?"

"Oh, yeah."

"He's, ahh... pretty special. He'll protect you and the kids, Sophia. If you need help, you won't find a better man."

Sophia's heart swelled with emotion. Sissy was right. There was no better man. At least, not for Sophia.

"Yep. He's a keeper. Talk soon. Bye." She sat for a few moments and let her imagination run rampant with the memories of their latest time together.

Heart lighter, heading for the kitchen, she plugged in the kettle and made sure it had enough water for several cups of coffee. Feeling in the need of a stimulant to be able to help her through this nightmare, she turned and surveyed the work of psychopaths who took enjoyment in hurting others.

Feeling dirty just being in the same room, she put on a pair of gloves, swallowed the disgust, and got busy.

Chapter Forty-four

Stasia sat in the car, her face covered in worry and her hands agitated. Keeping his eyes on the busy highway, Sam quickly glanced her way and then back to the traffic.

"What's wrong, Stasia? You look upset."

"I'm worried Ellie is angry. For me leaving this way. In middle of day. We had plans for children. To draw with them."

"I know, and I'm sorry I had to take you away. But we need your help to find your friend."

"You mean Maria?"

"Yes. You called her a few days ago, and she answered, right? We need you to do that again, but this time I want my guy to put a trace on the call."

"Won't they listen and find me again?"

"No. We'll be making the call from Starbucks downtown so even if they are watching, it won't matter."

Fear covering her features, Stasia held her stomach as if she suffered from pain. "Why do you need me to do this now?"

"I'd never ask you if it wasn't imperative. Look, Stasia, they've moved everyone out of the house where they were keeping you. We need you to find out where they went."

He pulled in close to the café and parked the car. Then he turned to her. "We want to help your friends, Stasia, but we can't if we don't have any idea where to go."

"I think they think I will call Maria again." She thought for a minute and added, "So... won't they take her phone?"

"It makes sense, yes. But if they are expecting you to call her again, they might not. They need to find you, Stasia. You know that. You're a loose end and could tell someone about their business. They can't take any chances."

Stasia looked at Sam, her eyes filling with tears. "The fear, it will never be gone, Sam, I know, right? Always,   I worry   someone could... could recognize me. How can I believe Stasia is good enough to be with Barney and family? If they find out secret... how... how dirty I am, they would be very, very angry."

Sam had no idea young Stasia would react like this to his request, but he couldn't blame her. Not at all. It would take years of counseling for most people to deal with the situation she'd found herself trapped in. He could tell her a million times she was the one wronged, the victim of adult cruelty, but she'd lived in the dirt, as she called it, for too long to have it wash off easily.

He turned to her and gathered her hands so she couldn't pull away. "Sophia told them about your situation the night before you went to work with them. They knew what had happened to you, and they're as infuriated about the treachery of those men as Sophia and I are. They're good people, Stasia, and what they care about is how you treat their kids and behave with them."

His words made the tears spill over. And Stasia's expression cleared when a glorious smile scattered the distress. "They know?"

"Yes, they do. Their reaction was wanting to show you there are good people in the world too."

"I'm so happy. You can't know, living lies, not telling truth. It's horrible. Ellie is so kind, I want to talk about my family with her."

"I bet they'll be pleased to hear all about your father and brothers and sisters. But for now, let's get this thing done, so I can get you back home in time to see Sophia off on her visit with Ellie's cousin."

Once they went up the flight of stairs to get to the Starbuck's entry, Sam saw David in the far corner of the veranda. He steered Stasia into the café so she could choose a drink and a treat if she wanted, and then they joined David who had his equipment spread over the table. He also had the largest glass they sold filled with a fruit drink and a plate with two huge pieces of coffee cake, a big bite out of one.

After he introduced them, David took out a cheap burner phone and asked Stasia for Maria's number. "Is she the only one who will answer?"

"I don't know. She did before. Would you rather I call Pavel? I know his number too."

David looked at Sam and then back to her. "Is he one of the others there?"

"Yes. We came on same ship together. He is two years older and different. But I don't care. I like him. He is kind."

Again, David looked over at Sam but didn't say a word. He just waited for orders.

Sam played it out in his head. If Maria did answer, chances were they'd either be listening or taping the call. But just maybe, they wouldn't be expecting Stasia to have memorized the number for one of the others. It was worth a try.

"Okay, Stasia. Give us Pavel's number, and if it's not him who answers, let David take the phone. He'll pretend to be a wrong number."

He then looked at David and asked, "You memorized how to ask for a person in Greek?"

"Yes, I called Sophia like you said to, and she coached me." Dave rambled off a sentence in the language and sounded authentic.

"Who were you asking for?"

"I think I asked for a taxi?"

"You think? Let's hope those guys aren't Greek, or they'll know it's a ruse."

David grinned. "I practiced all morning. Even called a number and got Anne a cab earlier."

Sam laughed. "Okay then, let's try."

David wrote down the info Stasia gave him, and then he pressed those numbers into the phone now attached to his equipment. It rang three times before they heard a young male voice, hesitant, sounding scared yet very abrupt. "What? They wanted me to stay. They said they would pay more."

"Pavel? Is that you?"

Silence followed, and then he spoke, excitement beginning to show in the awakening tone. "Who is this?"

"Stasia. I need to talk to you."

"Oh God, Stasia. Are you alright? They told us that you'd had an accident. That you were... dead." The last word held all the horror of his belief.

"No. No, I'm just hiding. I need to know something. Where they move you to. You're not at same house now."

"It's not far. Maybe a mile closer to town, but I think it's on the same highway. It's a white house, with a red-tiled roof. There's a big barn in the yard that's furnished. They organize parties to be held there. Crazy parties. I hate them. Tell me where you are. I'll run away too, and we can be together."

"I cannot say, Pavel. But I call soon. Thank you my friend. I love you. Bye."

"Bye." The choked, sad word hung in the void.

Sam saw Stasia use her napkin to wipe her eyes. He hated to see such a pretty young girl so damn sad... and with good reason.

Jesus, life was unfair to the unlucky.

Chapter
Forty-five

Sophia breathed a sigh of relief when she returned to the hotel and found that Stasia and Sam weren't there. Obviously, something had come up. She needed to find out what had happened without sharing her earlier troubles. Sam had enough on his plate right now. Besides, she still didn't want him calling off her date with Manos.

Making up her mind, unable to handle not knowing why he'd taken Stasia to town, she called him to find he was on his way back and Stasia was with him. Now she had her reason for not saying anything about the break-in. No way she wanted Stasia feeling guilty about her Yaya's house being vandalized.

"Hi, sweetie. I tried calling you a few times earlier, but you didn't answer." His voice sounded wonderful after the strain of her day. The endearment made her grin too. No one had ever called her sweetie. She sensed he tried not to accuse her of ignoring his calls, especially while he had the kid sitting there listening to what they said. Good. That worked in her favor.

"I'm sorry, Sam. I was cleaning out Yaya's house, packing things, running in and out, and I left my phone in the kitchen. I saw there were messages just as I arrived here at the hotel, so I'm returning your calls. What's up?"

"A few things we need to discuss. Will you still be there when we arrive? We're about twenty minutes out."

"No. Sorry. It's going to take me longer to drive to Manos's place, so I figured to leave soon. Is there something I need to know?" She heard the frustration he didn't try to hide. Something happened.

"We found out that they moved the captives out of the house. David's been watching and figured they've been slowly relocating to another place. Then last night, no one returned. I guess they've been shifting a few at a time, but now they have them all at the new location."

"Gentle Jesus, we can't catch a break." Disgust showed plainly in the words and her tone.

"Something's happened?"

The man had radar for Chrissakes. "No, I'm fine. I just feel bad for you and the others. What's going to happen now?"

"Everything's in order. Stasia helped us find the

new place, and we're able to make the changes. It'll all go through as planned. As long as you're sure that your end is still a go."

"As far as I'm concerned it is. I talked to Manos earlier and he mentioned me taking the kids to Marmaris tomorrow, so I figure we're good there too. All you need to do once we're clear and the plane is in the air is coordinate the arrests to happen all at once. Thank goodness the boat arrives early enough for me to take the morning flight. And... you need to make it happen when everyone is at the house so no one can warn the others."

"I know. It's all arranged. Now you just have to survive this evening. I still don't like you going there alone."

"Yeah. I kinda feel the same way. But it's worth spending time with the menace as long as we get what we need. See you soon." Before she hung up his last words came through and made her feel slightly sick – like a premonition she should pay attention to.

"Be safe, Sophia."

Lord love a duck, she hated when her insides reacted with such a surge of queasy anticipation.

***

Dressed in a colorful, flowing flowered top and tight white pants, her high-heeled sandals decorated with a mixture of silver and pearl beads, she arrived at Mano's home and watched the gates open to her vehicle as if he'd been waiting for her arrival.

When she saw him coming forward to greet her, the worry subsided somewhat, and she almost felt silly for letting her imagination run amuck. Goodness, she needed to get her cool back before he sensed her reluctance.

She drove the car close to the sprawling house and checked all around to get the lay of the land. The white house had been recently painted and looked fresh, as did the blue shutters on every window and the wrap-around veranda. It was a sprawling older home, but that added to the attraction.

The out-buildings were in the middle of renovations other than one exception. The place closest to the house looked brand new, and she wondered if it was the famous stable he'd bragged about the other evening. There were three ponies in a fenced-in paddock attached to the log building. Two were small and those cuties were gamboling together, whereas the larger one was over in the corner with his back turned.

Reaching for her small handbag with her weapon nestled inside, she slipped it over her shoulder and exited the car quickly so there wouldn't be any excuse for him to touch her when he finally got closer.

"Hello, Sophia. You're right on time." He approached and leaned in to kiss her cheek, which she allowed. But to stop him from moving in too close, she put out her hands so he had no option but to take them and stand back.

"Hi, Manos. What a beautiful home! No wonder you were bragging about it the other day. It's gorgeous. And I thought Corinne had a lovely view. This makes hers look like a backdrop to a forties movie." She turned in the direction where the cliff overlooked a vista of mountains, green trees, and the ocean beyond. To the right, the city could be seen in the distance with the picturesque blue waters behind, melding into the sky. No doubt, the sight after dark would be breathtaking.

"I'm happy to show you my little paradise. Come with me. The stables are my pride and joy. They just delivered a new arrival today; one I've been waiting for. This thoroughbred is an incredible runner and is here to perform his... ahh, male duties with my little mare. She's fast and sturdy and will be a good match for him."

The visual image from his words was disturbing. "I thought that was all done by injections nowadays."

"Yes, of course that happens. But the Jockey Club requires Stallions to 'live cover' a mare for its foal to become a registered thoroughbred racehorse. I bought him in England and had him shipped here. Don't worry, Sophia, we'll help mother nature take its course."

A sickening thought took hold, and Sophia

couldn't shake it loose. No doubt, this whack-a-doodle liked watching small mares being overpowered by a hot-blooded, attacking, fully-engorged thoroughbred.

Manos continued his story, not noticing her reaction, "Rambo arrived today and is having difficulty settling in. Would you mind if we checked on him?"

"Of course not. I love horses." She let Manos encircle her waist as he guided her to the open doorway that led to the stalls. She hadn't been in a lot of stables before, but anyone with an eye to detail could tell he'd spared no expense. Three other horses had poked their heads over their enclosures, and all seemed agitated by the screaming fury of their newest roommate. There at the end of the room, a larger pen imprisoned the unhappy newcomer.

As soon as they entered, Alexandro spotted them and came running. "Papa, Rambo is a monster. No one can get close to him to calm him down. I'm afraid he's going to injure himself."

It was obvious that no one had the expertise to handle the savage and until someone stepped in, he would keep spiraling. "Stay back, son. I've told you he isn't like the others." Manos pointed to an older man who held the stallion's reins, trying to force him into his stall. "Barak, why haven't you taken control? He's escalating."

"I've never worked with a Thoroughbred like

him, boss. He's not behaving the way most horses do. Everything I've tried just makes him worse."

While the men were talking, Sophia happened to see Alexandro approach from the back and the horse sensing someone there, kicked out. She had just enough time to grab the boy and shove him behind her. From the corner of her eye, she saw Manos reach for the rifle they had mounted on the wall and lift it to his shoulder.

She called out, her voice singsong and gentle, "Manos, wait."

Slowly, carefully, she began to step around the animal so he could see her and not feel nervous. "Hey, pretty boy, you wanna kick a lady? I didn't think so."

She stopped where she was and let him get used to her presence. His ears were pulled back and, she hoped it was because he was listening to her voice. His switching tail made her nervous as did his continually pawing the ground. Tall, close to six feet of streamlined muscle, the black coat glistened with sweat that she could smell from the exhausted beast.

Stilled, like a picture in time, she sensed not just anger from the poor animal, there was fear of the unknown there too. It was the only reason she held out her hand and kept her voice low. "Come on, baby. You need to calm down and let Barak look after you. You're tired and unhappy, I know. But it'll be better once you settle in. That's the good boy."

The horse turned her way and stared at her. His screams stopped and so did his pawing and stamping. Finally, he lowered his head and let Barak lead him into the stall they had readied for him.

Manos threw the gun down on a pile of straw in disgust, grabbed the boy she'd pushed behind her and shoved him toward the house angrily. "Go. I'll deal with you later." Then he came to her. "Sophia, that was incredible. I thought you said you haven't been around a lot of horses."

"I haven't. I just treated him like any animal who was scared from being taken away from his home, traveling for God knows how long confined in an unfamiliar place on some ship, and then forced to deal with strangers. No doubt, he'll settle in time. This is a beautiful home for the lucky horse."

He closed in, his intentions plain. Reaching for her, she again gave him her hands and shook his in a playful way. "This girl needs a drink. It's been an unforgettable beginning to the evening."

Catching her cheerful manner, he pulled her right hand to his mouth so he could put a kiss there and went along with her request. "You're right. Where are my manners? It's just watching you standing up against that beast, a slender creature like you willing to take on that large animal and save my boy has my utmost respect and appreciation. You were splendid. Beautiful! No wonder Rambo listened."

"Stop! You're embarrassing me." Sophia looked to the ground so he couldn't read the distaste that overcame her from his boasting.

"You're right. I'm sorry. We'll go to the veranda to have that cocktail, and you shall tell me all about your terrible day."

When they arrived, the twins came to greet her, and she let down her guard. "Hi Jack and Casey. I'm so glad you want to come with me and Peter tomorrow to Marmaris. We'll have a lot of fun. Make sure and bring hats and a change of clothes, okay? I'll bring the rest of the gear like suntan lotion, water and snacks."

Both the kids were jumping in place from the excitement. Their questions came hot and heavy, but Manos put a stop to their barrage within a few minutes. "Okay, okay. Let Sophia have some peace now. You'll see her soon enough in the morning."

Not sure she understood, but the sneaky feeling couldn't be ignored, "Aren't they staying with us? I thought you told me at the barbecue you wanted me to have dinner with you and your children? I was looking forward to getting to know them more before tomorrow."

Suave as a snake-oil salesman, he passed her the glass of champagne and sat close by... too close. "The two little ones are always in bed by seven. They're up early in the morning and tire themselves out. And... I'm not happy with Alex right now. It's best he stay away from me until I calm down."

She'd seen the anger in his handling of the boy earlier, but hoped he'd have spoken to him, explaining what he'd done had been foolish and dangerous. In fact, since they'd come into the house, she'd expected him to excuse himself and deal with the incident. But to leave the kid hanging, waiting for punishment, was cruel and unnecessary.

"I'm fine if you want to go and have a little talk with him before we eat. I'm sure he's anxious. And, I could sit here and look at this view forever."

"No. I have no wish to give up any of my time with you. He'll be fine. It's best he stays in his room." Manos smiled, relaxing back into his chair and lifted his crystal fluted glass. "Now, tell me what you finally decided to do at your grandmother's house. Did you call the police?"

***

The evening continued in the same way as it started. Him coming on to her, and her backing off just enough to keep him interested, yet not really giving him more than she could stomach. Comparing him to a man like Sam made the whole thing more difficult. But, all she had to do was get through these few hours, and it would be clear sailing after that.

"I had the cook prepare us my favorite Greek dish called Pastitsio. Have you tasted it before?"

"Of course. It's one of my favorites too. Who doesn't like baked pasta with ground beef and béchamel sauce?"

"Then you do recognize it. I'm glad. She left it for us in the oven and the table is set. All I have to do is bring everything to the dining room, and we can enjoy."

"Couldn't we eat out here? It's so perfect." The breeze had picked up and the odors of hot sunshine, salty ocean and sweet scents from surrounding flowering bushes battled for supremacy. If only she could close her eyes, let the beauty seep in and forget who she was with. Regrettably, she still had a role to play.

Manos tried to sound like he felt badly, but she sensed he really didn't. "The evening bugs will start attacking very soon. It's best we eat indoors."

Giving up the feeling of the unconfined safety, she agreed. "Let me help you then."

Manos smiled his approval and graciously accepted her assistance. "Good, we'll do it together. You can mix the salad."

When she stood to walk inside, he caught her off guard at the door and turned to take her in his arms. Not able to maneuver easily because of the doorway, she let him hug her, but kept her mouth away from his searching lips. Instead, she teasingly suggested they needed to eat before their favorite food became overdone.

And thank God for small mercies, he pawed her

back, nuzzled her neck, then freed her. "You're right. This is the time to eat."

They spent quite a while conversing and enjoying the delicious food. The cook had outdone herself with stuffed grape leaves called Dolmades, and she'd also made Tomatokeftedes a kind of Tomato Fritters seen in Santorini. Then she'd finished off her menu with a dessert called Feta Me Meli, a feta cheese wrapped with pastry and coated with a honey sauce.

"This is some of the best food I've ever tasted in Rhodes, Manos. Everything was delicious."

"I like my food, I admit it. And when I went to a restaurant along the beach near the Palace Hotel and tasted such heavenly dishes, I offered the woman a job instantly. Only she couldn't leave her business with her husband, so she suggested the daughter she trained to come work for me instead. Nan lives near and comes four days a week."

"She's worth every penny you pay her. I'm afraid I stuffed myself." Knowing it was time for her to reach out to Sam and let him know things were progressing as planned, Sophia slid her chair back just as Manos leaned toward her. Pretending she didn't notice, she asked him to point her to the bathroom and taking her purse, she followed his directions. "Come to the family room when you're ready, darling. I'll just leave this mess for the morning."

Heading to where he pointed, she passed an

open door and spied young Alex propped on his bed, a book of horses in his hands. When he saw her, a guilty look appeared before he replaced it with a smirk. "Did you enjoy your dinner?"

"Yes, I did. What about you? Do you like Greek food?"

"What food? My father is mad at me. There will be no food for me tonight."

Instant fury flooded. "That's not going to happen." She reversed direction and headed back to the dining room in time to see Manos in angry conversation with another man. "Manos, Alex—" They turned, and everyone froze. She couldn't back up in time to unsee the person even if she tried. Unfortunately, it was the same guy who'd attacked her at the beach the night she'd saved Stasia. The very asshole who'd shot out the combination on her Yaya's closet door the evening before.

No one moved. Not knowing how the hell she could play this scene – every protective instinct ramping to high – her mind searched for an answer to the dilemma; a way to escape the sudden danger.

Chapter
Forty-six

Sam waited for her call. Doing so didn't sit well with him. In fact, it drove him crazy. He kept checking that his phone was turned on, or if there was enough battery and the sound was on high. His anxiety levels were off the charts. Crazy broad! How did she imagine he was going to behave when she'd told him to look for her around ten and it was now midnight? He thought of every reason for her being late. He'd even sunk as low as hoping she had a flat tire, yet knowing she'd have called him if that was the reason for her delay.

Barney had visited for a short while and left saying, "You're making me crazy. I feel as nervous as I was when Ellie gave birth to Peter. I hate it when my stomach churns, and I feel like I'm about to puke any minute. For Chrissakes man, calm down. Sophia's fine. She's an agent with the FBI and can handle herself."

"Then why hasn't she called?"

"Could be she's having so much fun with the kids, she's forgotten the time. Nah! That's dumb. They'd be in bed." Barney's grin slipped. "I'm no help, am I?"

Sam glared. "Not particularly, no."

"Okay, I'll leave you. Time to hit the sack. It's been a long day, and I have no doubt it's going to be an exciting one tomorrow. I suggest you grab some shuteye too."

Sam waved Barney off and wondered how the stupid bastard thought he would be getting any goddamn *shuteye* when everything inside him screamed something was wrong.

Bounding to his feet, he reached for his car keys, checked to see if his weapon was safe in the leg holster, and headed for the car.

That's it! I don't give a flying fuck if she's mad at me or not, I'm going there.

***

Ellie let the curtains slide and turned to Barney. "Okay, you can come to bed now. He's gone after her."

Chapter Forty-seven

Sophia pointed at the man next to Manos. "What's he doing here? That's the same son of a bitch who's been my nightmare since I arrived."

Manos moved into her space, and her Spidey senses told her to run, get the hell out, but she just couldn't give up now. "Manos, I'm telling you, this guy is bad news. What does he want?"

"It seems that he's followed you here and is asking about you."

"About me?" Stalling, she tried a fake chuckle and stepped forward aggressively. "Me? I bet he's the jerk who wrecked my Yaya's house that I spent all day cleaning. Why the hell does he think he can follow me?" She pointed at the man standing as still as a statue, seemingly unsure of his next move, waiting for direction. "What the hell do you want from me?"

Manos gestured for the prick to answer, but his

eyes seemed to send a message to be careful of what was said.

Asshole leaned forward, temper sparking, "You have my ward, a Russian bi-girl called Anastasia. I paid her father for her to work for me, and she's run off. You helped her. I want to know... where is she?"

Sophia looked first to Manos and then answered, "You terrified her so badly last night that she ran off. I don't have a clue where she is."

"She called one of the others today. He told us. I want her back."

"Others?" The word spilled out before she could bite it off. Shit! She'd said the one thing that opened pandora's box. *Shit!*

Sophia watched Manos in her peripheral vision and saw him reaching the same conclusion. "Take her!"

His order left her no choice.

She ran.

Heading to the French doors on the veranda, she pushed through them and ran straight to the dimly lit stable. Her sandals didn't help. When she bent over to undo the back straps, her purse dropped and rolled away into the dark. *Fuck!* There was no time to retrieve it before they closed in. She took off again.

Maybe the old man in the stable, Barak, would be able to stop Manos and his pal from doing whatever they had in mind. Or maybe she could get him to call 911. She barged in through the closed doors and found the place empty, the horses enclosed for the night. The only animal still somewhat free was Rambo. He'd been put into his stall, but he hadn't been shut in completely. Barak must have sensed that the horse had enough of that on the ship and had left him able to move around rather than tethering him to a wall.

Panic hung over her and the horse must have sensed it. He began to fret like before, neighing his disgruntles, shaking his head to let her know this intrusion didn't sit well with him. Taking a minute to soothe him, she whispered, "I'm sorry, baby. I know you're unhappy. But trust me, that makes two of us."

She needed to hide. But where? She heard the two men opening the door. Jesus, Mary, and Joseph, the screaming in her ears was making her crazy. Then she realized it wasn't nerves. It was Rambo. He was *really* not happy.

Looking everywhere, knowing there was no safe place to be where they couldn't reach her, she did the one thing that might save her life. She wriggled into the stall, moving around Rambo, and blessed her luck that he sidestepped and pranced, but he didn't attack.

Manos came forward but not too close. "Come out from there, Sophia. Rambo could crush you against the wall."

"He won't unless you provoke him. Go away."

"You're being silly. We will talk this through, and no one needs to get hurt. It's all a mistake. You know that, right?"

Wishing she hadn't dropped her purse, she wondered if he could still be played. If she could get out of this predicament without Sam's plans being interrupted.

"I want you to trust me. I'll send Douglas away and it'll be just you and me."

His words created a disgusting image. "I'm fine here with Rambo. Just go away." Suddenly the old man, Barak, appeared at the opening of the stable and rushed to where Manos was standing. Doug slipped into the shadows and Barak didn't see him. He had his eyes glued to the fretting horse.

"Bôs! What's happening in here? You're making Rambo nervous. Move back."

Before he could answer, Doug appeared, swung a shovel, and clipped Barak on the back of his head. The man dropped to the ground; the sickening noise of the steel meeting skin resonating in the sudden quiet. Sophia felt sick to her stomach, and Rambo reacted to the increased tension surrounding him. He began running back and forth in his pen, leaping, kicking at the fencing, yet always shielding her as if he sensed he was her protection.

From her angle, she saw the glazed hatred in his eyes, the determination to be free so he could attack. No amount of words spoken softly altered his mood.

Knowing they'd passed the point of no return, Manos lost the cajoling sound from his tone and spoke with freezing authority, "Sophia, I will give you three minutes to make up your mind. Come out. Or I will shoot the fucking horse." Then he lost it on Doug and screamed his order. "You fool! Did you kill him?"

Doug scrambled to his knees by the old man and checked for a pulse. "He's alive. Do you want I should kill him?"

"No, you idiot. Get him to his quarters and dump him on the bed. He didn't see you. And since I was in front of him the whole time, he'll know I never hurt him. I'll tell him it was a horse thief after Rambo. He heard the horse going crazy, so it's believable. Then bring the SUV here to the stable."

Once Doug left, Manos backed away from where Sophia still hid and made his belligerent tone less quarrelsome. "Come now, Sophia. We can talk."

"I'll come if you stay by the door. Rambo is getting worse. Step back."

Manos did back up a few feet and crossed his arms. "Fine, have it your way. Now get out of that stall before he kills you."

Sophia angled herself over to the one spot where she hoped, with any luck, she could reach the stable rifle before he understood her plans. Rambo didn't like her moving. He pawed the ground and snorted to emphasize his dislike of her leaving him. "It's okay, baby. Calm down. Good boy."

Once she cleared the fencing, Manos headed toward her. At the last minute, she veered away, reached for the rifle, and held it pointed his way. "Stop, Manos. Don't move you scum-sucking son of a bitch."

"Tsk tsk, such language from a lady?"

"Maybe a lady wouldn't use those kinds of words, but an FBI agent wouldn't hesitate. Let's go."

"Where?"

"You're going to get Doug to come join us, and then I'm going to call the police."

"I have joined you." Doug's voice came from behind her, and she knew then why a stupid grin had lit up Manos's face.

Without hesitation, she swung the rifle and shot the gun from the asshole's hand, this time making sure she hit skin and bone. What she didn't expect was to hear Sam's voice behind Manos warning him to stop where he was. Only the idiot didn't listen. He ran to her, grabbed the rifle barrel, and swung her around so her back would be toward Sam.

Fed up from playing with the jerk all evening, sick and tired of hiding her skills, she kept hold of her weapon but brought her knee up and drove it into his lower stomach, loving the squeal of discomfort he let loose.

Doug, seeing his boss in trouble, lifted his gun from the ground with his left hand, and took aim. He shot off the first round and would have fired again if Sophia hadn't shoved Manos at him, giving her the perfect cover to run behind one of the stalls.

Sam joined her and spoke, "You alright?"

"Yeah. What are you doing here? I thought we agreed I'd handle tonight."

"Yeah. We agreed you'd call me too. Guess my chauvinistic tendencies got the better of me. It's the old thing – you didn't call, you didn't write... Sue me."

Grinning, Sophia just patted his arm. "Poor baby. I'll make it up to you. Now what are we going to do here? These guys aren't giving up easily. And there's a few hours before the raids will be happening. We can't let them go."

"Nope. Not going to happen. Look, I'll go around the back and find the door the big guy came through, maybe sneak up behind them."

"Okay. I'm fine here. In the meantime, I'll shoot a few rounds to keep them occupied."

Sophia let loose three bullets and sat back on her heels to listen for Sam's entry. In the meantime, Rambo had gone way past any thought of calming down. He screamed his anger and ran from one end of the pen to the other, stopping to paw the air, bucking, his head swinging from side to side.

He hadn't liked her leaving him, and he liked it less that bullets were flying and those men were posing a threat.

When Sam appeared at the back door, Sophia waited for him to let her know he'd caught them unaware, only that's not what happened. Tired of waiting, Manos now held Doug's gun and stepped into the open with the muzzle against the big man's head.

Forcing him into the open, he shouted, "You drop that rifle, Sophia. And tell your friend to come out, or I'll shoot this idiot – right here, right now."

Sophia saw Sam step into the lighted area, and she watched as he lowered his gun. "Okay, I'm here. You don't have any quarrel with Sophia, let her go."

Sophia knew that they'd come to the end of the final round. That for Manos, it was now or never. She'd seen that look many times in the eyes of a killer. They reached a pinnacle where they were willing to do whatever it took to win. She lifted the rifle, took aim, and made a once in a lifetime shot... even for her.

The bullet hit the small, red button that was the automatic gate opener to Rambo's pen, and he flew into the stable, kicking and pawing and taking his fury out on the men who'd made him the most nervous. Those who now blocked his way to freedom.

The hoof that clipped Manos in the head, put him down instantly. Then the horse did a number on Doug before Sam yelled, waved his arms, and scared him away. The crazed beast finally turned to Sophia who ran to open the door to freedom. He flashed past her, hightailing it for the fresh grass he smelled in the far paddock. He cleared the fence and ran to the end where he heaved in disgust at the treatment he'd just endured.

Chapter Forty-eight

The ambulance came in record time, but it was too late for Manos. Rambo's powerful hoof had killed him instantly. Doug was another matter. Terribly wounded, but alive, the ambulance attendants were able to treat him as well as Barak, who still lived though was in bad shape. By the time Sam had called for backup at the ranch and everything that could be done was in place, he'd also contacted Maureen, who would be arriving on the next flight.

In the meantime, Sophia, who'd always kept the goal in mind of finding the information Bruner had specifically asked for, searched the desk in Manos's office. She looked for any information on hostages still in route. She went through the papers strewn on top of his desk and then she flipped though the ones he'd piled in drawers.

Nothing!

Frustrated, knowing she had little time before

the locals tied down the scene, she went to the closet where he had shelves full of files and looked into each one trying to find any information.

Again... nothing.

Blasted hell! She wanted the name of that ship and the container number Bruner asked her to find. The one holding the trafficked young people due in any day. If they could intercept the landing and release the new batch of hostages, she'd be able to let go of the horrible visual she'd been living with ever since he'd told her about the container.

She dropped into Manos's chair, and her troubled gaze drifted to the photograph of his house with the kids in front that sat on the corner of his desk. That's when she noticed the folded calendar he had next to the frame. Could it be that simple?

Hands shaking, she scooped the item up and saw he'd circled dates and even scrawled messages in the boxes under certain ones that were important. And there it was. He'd marked the next day and the time with a name of the shipping company and there was also a number. Quickly, she took a photo with her phone and sent it to Bruner with a note for him to check into it. With her fingers crossed, she followed Sam's voice calling from the other room.

Barney had arrived. They quickly organized the children, intending the twins to go with Barney and stay with his family where they would be cared for until their mother flew into Rhodes the next day.

But Alexandro was another matter altogether. He wanted to remain at the ranch, in his father's home, and when Barney invited him to get into his vehicle with the others, he put up a huge battle and stomped away, his grief terrible to see.

Sophia went to comfort the boy and decided not to beat around the bush. It needed to be talked out. "Your father's death was purely an accident, Alex. We couldn't settle Rambo; you saw how he behaved yesterday."

"But how did he get loose? Why wasn't he in the pen? My father wouldn't have let him run free."

"He didn't. I did. The horse was going crazy being penned in the stall. I wanted to let him go so he wouldn't damage himself." She didn't add the truth that her intentions had been to create a distraction. "I didn't know he would attack and unintentionally kill your father. It was an accident."

Alexandro must have heard the sincerity in her voice which made him accept the truth. "It was an accident." He turned to her and revealed the anguish he felt inside. "Last night, my father was angry with me."

"He was frightened that you could have been injured, and he was right. Rambo might have hurt you too. All I heard was a father's fear for his son's safety. A father who loved that son, was proud of him and wanted to protect him. He bragged about you during dinner, about how smart you were and such a good rider. Alex, Manos loved you dearly."

In truth, it had been Sophia who had brought up the children during their meal. The bragging father had termed his remarks in such a way as boasting about his teaching skills, making their accomplishments his rather than the children's. In her eyes, it made him appear even less of a good father, but she hadn't pointed it out. Just encouraged him to keep talking.

Alexandro continued, "He was going to keep me with him. He told me."

"Of course, he wanted to keep you. You made him proud."

"But now, I can't stay. I must go back to my mother. She didn't want him to take me away. They fought. I heard them. But he insisted."

"We'll contact her for you. And we'll make sure that you get home safely. Go with Barney and the others for now."

"Will I see you again?"

Sophia hugged the hesitant boy to her and nodded, "Of course. I'll be there soon."

Once Barney waved goodbye, Sophia met up with Sam who'd finished dealing with the ambulance and the coroner. "What's happening next, Sam? Did they arrest the Police Commander and the Mayor so they couldn't warn the others at the house?"

"Yes, thanks to Yanis. He organized the council to approve of an interim person in charge. They've restrained both under house arrest for now. But it's decided we must move in to save the others. Those assholes will be wondering about Doug, and we can't let them find out what went down here with their boss." Sam looked into her eyes, his unsure and wary. "I want to be there."

"Of course." She had full intentions of coming along and worried that Sam might act like a worried boyfriend rather than a colleague in the field. She should have known better.

"Are you coming?"

"I wouldn't miss it for the world."

On the way, driving like a race car driver, Sam seemed preoccupied.

"What's wrong?" Sophia couldn't stand all the words floating through the air unspoken.

"Nothing's wrong. Not now. You're here beside me. I can breathe again."

Aww. Now that's what a girl needed to hear. And she knew exactly what he meant. After everything happened so fast in the stable, just knowing he was safe had her dropping to her knees, weak and shaken.

When life spins out of control as it just had, one sees what's important, and for her knowing Sam hadn't been injured by the wild stallion too had been a blessing.

"Here we are. The house is just a bit further up

the road."

Sophia saw a black SUV parked near two police cars in the early morning dusk, and she recognized Anne Carmen and David. Marc approached on the other side and met up with Sam. "They sent three other officers to step in and take over procedures after things had been locked down. Are you ready?"

"And the other places are still a go? Amsterdam too?"

"As far as I know, it's all lined up."

Both her and Sam retrieved their weapons and moved in behind the officers. After the other excitement they'd survived, this action seemed low-key and boring. The guard at the door had fallen asleep and was surrounded and hauled away before he could warn those inside.

The lock on the door gave way to the first drive of the ramming device and they were inside. They swept through the house in a matter of seconds, arresting Fedrika and the other two jailers.

Soon, they'd gathered all of the fourteen bewildered hostages together and explained they would soon be free. Sam approached one young man. "Are you Pavel?"

After being studied for a few minutes, the fellow answered, "Yes."

"Good. I wanted you to know that it's because of you we were able to find this house. You shared information with Stasia and she's with us. She will be happy to see you. Where's Maria?"

Pavel pointed to a smaller person curled in a ball in one of the chairs. She had a cut on her lip, her hair was a matted mess, and she seemed to be in shock. "I will tell her she will see Stasia soon. It will give her something to live for."

Sam patted Pavel's back and answered, "We're taking you all to a beautiful resort now, and every last one of you will be looked after until we sort out your papers and destinations. Don't be afraid. Tell the others. My name is Sam, and I will be taking care of you all."

Finally, after searching and retrieving documents and whatever the hostages wished to keep, the place was secured. Everyone could breathe a sigh of relief that no word of their invasion and resulting arrests would get out.

***

By the time Sophia and Sam returned to Barney's, both were imagining hot showers and a soft bed. They were done for. Which didn't mean they wouldn't be ready for the mess of things waiting for them once they woke up. But at the moment, they needed to recover after the night's gruesome events.

Sophia entered the luxurious bathroom enclosure, stood under the rainforest showerhead and let the warmth drain away all her tears. The shock and fear she'd survived earlier had been crammed into the background. Now was the time to process. With her eyes closed, totally immersed, she didn't see or even hear Sam until his hand holding a bar of soap began a pathway of delight down her back.

Stunned, not sure how she felt about his intrusion, she stiffened. His husky voice whispered the words that let her relax back into his arms and let him see her truth. That it mattered to her when a man died, no matter how he'd behaved in life.

"I love you, Special Agent Sophia Dunne. No matter what happens, I'm sorry for what you had to go through earlier tonight."

She turned into his arms and relaxed her restraints, cried hard and let the huge ball of pain break into tiny pieces she could handle a little at a time.

Chapter
Forty-nine

Sam could see how affected Sophia was from the evening's events, that she'd jammed all the stress behind her while they still had work to do. That's how people in the business dealt with each conflict.

He understood. Many times, he'd gone along a similar path – waiting until he could close his door before allowing the misery to show itself.

Understanding her, knowing his heart savored the knowledge that it had found her, he gratefully accepted the blessing. She'd be the perfect partner for a lifetime position as his one and only.

This strong woman didn't take anything for granted or shrug off the painful happenings she'd suffered because of her job. He loved that about her. Hell, he loved her.

When the words burst free in the shower, her reaction had been everything he'd hoped for. She'd nestled close to let him soothe her, and then she'd whispered in return, "You're all that matters."

He'd lifted her in his arms then and turned off the water, dried her with the fluffy towels and placed her in the bed next to him where he held her in his arms while they both slept. It was hours later that his hungry lips and tender hands showed her just how much she really meant to a man who'd been a loner for too many years.

***

A few hours later, Marc called Sam with the updates on their other stakeouts, and thankfully, all had gone as planned. Their only outstanding case now was the container full of the last detainees Manos had organized. His partners stateside had all been arrested thanks to Bruner who had reached out to various other FBI offices to step in. And when the shipment arrived, there would be a team waiting for them at the New York and New Jersey wharf.

He felt a huge relief to know that all those hostages would be free, many to return home. Maybe a few would luck out with jobs in places better than they'd left.

Like Anastasia, who would now have a choice to stay and work for Barney, send money home as planned originally or give up and return to her family. No one could blame her if that's what she decided to do. Although, Sam would bet his last dollar she'd grab this opportunity Ellie and Barney had presented to her with both hands.

And if she didn't, he'd make sure she returned to school and her family didn't suffer because they lacked her wages. There were always ways if you knew people in as many places as he did.

Chapter Fifty

Later the next night, Sam had picked up Maureen at the airport. She now held her babies close, both nestled in her arms on her lap and loving the attention. Sam felt such a relief to see them together that he didn't want to disrupt their reunion, but he had little time and still so much to process.

"Sis, I have to tell you a few things. Yanis had a lawyer look into Manos's affairs, and it seems that he owned the ranch outright and a number of other investments. Since you're the mother of his children, they want to know how you intend to handle his estate."

"It's all money from his ahh... murky business dealings, and we want no part of it. Let them set up a fund to help the poor hostages whose lives he's disrupted because of his crimes. Maybe start a trust for Alexandro's education. But I want nothing to do with it."

She couldn't have made it more plain how she felt. She turned to Sophia, "I can't thank you enough for being so kind to Jack and Casey. They've told me how excited they were about going to the circus with you. I think it gave them something to look forward to."

Sophia moved in on the trio on the couch and knelt in front so she would be even with the kids. "You know how we were going to go to the circus in Marmaris?"

Both kids nodded and both looked sad because of their lost treat.

"Well... I have a surprise for you. There is that exact circus just outside of Washington, and when we're home, we can have our day together. Do you still want me to take you?"

The kids leapt forward, their arms reaching for her, "Yes, please. Can we go?" Jack turned to Maureen and then his head swiveled to glare at Sophia, "My mom wants to come with us. She can, right?"

"Of course, your mother can come." Sophia caught Maureen's eye and got the tearful nod of agreement. "It's all settled. In three days, we'll be there and get into as much mischief as possible."

Casey piped up and pointing to a smiling Sam, she insisted, "Uncle Sam has to be with us. We want him to be there too. Can he, Mommy?"

Sam winked at Sophia, loving the special way

her mouth curled in the shy, side grin and whisked the tiny girl from her mother's arms to throw her high into air. "I wouldn't miss it for the world, button. Escorting all my beautiful girls to a circus where they sell cotton candy and corn dogs. Oh yeah! Count me in."

Afterword

Thank you so much for reading *Special Agent Sophia.*

I loved writing this very special story, and I hope you enjoyed reading it too. If so, I would ask you for a favor. Wherever you purchased this book, please take a few minutes and leave an honest review. Authors enjoy hearing that readers like their stories, and hopefully, others will read your words and choose to buy the book because of your sentiments.

My website at **http://mimibarbour.com** now has all my books listed with links to the various publishers to make it easy for you to return to where you bought the book and to find my other work.

While you're there, I'd really appreciate it if you would sign up for my newsletter so I can keep in touch. **http://bit.ly/MimiBNewsletter.** I only send out newsletters approximately twice a month. It's usually full of giveaways, contests and freebies, along with my personal news. (You have my word that your address will never be shared.)

Hugs, Mimi

Special Agent Murphy

Undercover FBI Book #8

AMAZON
by
Mimi Barbour

NYT & USA Today Best-selling author

It's Christmas in Washington, but not for one heartsick family

Agent Shane Murphy has a hard time believing his life could get so crazy. Because of a choice – one he'd make again – he loses his superiority in the FBI. Now he's forced to work surveillance with a rookie female yapper. And... gets caught up in the kidnapping of a sixteen-year-old that pulls at the heartstrings he keeps hidden.

Fighting the budding attraction for his new partner, he stresses his way through an escalating nightmare. How can he be so infatuated with a trouble-magnet female who drives like a granny and isn't able to hide her sensitive reactions when on the job?

Agent Kathleen Edwards does a lot of things her new partner dislikes, but what's a girl to do when a man ties her in knots and turns her into a chatterbox. Working to uncover the mystery of who kidnapped the Senator's daughter, and where they're holding her, continuous conflicts arise.

Working alongside an attractive realist whose high morals make him someone to live up to,

Kayti's heart doesn't stand a chance.

Praise:

Reviews for Special Agent Murphy:

"I enjoyed this story! It's a good addition to the "Undercover FBI" series of stand-alone stories. Passion ignites between partners. I love the characters and the plot is intriguing. It's entertaining and a good mix of action, suspense, passion, and romance. I look forward to reading what this author comes up with next." ~ **Reviewed by Mary**

"This is a great series! Great characters in each book and a storyline you'll love reading. Special Agent Murphy is a great addition to the series. You'll love the characters, the storyline is enjoyable to read and very well written."~ **Reviewed by buzymomof2**

"This book was so good and I have really been loving this series! Murphy and Kayti made such an amazing team, in and out of the field, and I loved that they seemed like an opposites attract couple with some amazing chemistry! Murphy is loyal, hard-working, shows a crusty side, but has a huge heart! And I really loved his protective nature when it came to those he loved. Kayti has a huge heart, a softer touch with those in need, but loved how she was like Wonder Woman when it came to kicking butt and wanting to protect others! I loved the case that they were assigned to, full of drama, mystery, and danger! This was a great romantic suspense book and I look forward to more from Ms. Barbour!" ~**Reviewed by Jessica N**

Chapter One - Special Agent Murphy

Murphy pulled into his driveway and saw his neighbor acting like an asshole again. It happened often, and Murphy was sick of it. He left the car, intending to ignore the fact that the kid was getting blasted.

"Little shit. You listen to me when I talk to you."

"When you make sense, maybe I will. Until then, back off and leave me alone. I'm not handing over any money, so give it up."

"I feed you, clothe you and put a fucking roof over your head. Then, when I ask for a few bucks, you act like I'm some mysterious thief trying to steal your future. Piss on your future, what about now? What about me? I need money."

"Then get off your lazy fat ass, get a job and earn some – like you've made me do."

Losing his shit, the older man suddenly turned into a crazy fool. He rushed at the boy, grabbed him by his arm and hauled back to punch. In earlier years, no doubt, he'd have connected, but now the boy was strong and filled with angry disgust. Rather than take the punishment, he yanked himself from the other's grasp, turned and started to leave.

Only he didn't see his dad pull off the piece of broken fence, whip it behind his back and swing full force.

If Murphy hadn't stepped out at that moment to haul the kid away, the board would have connected, and no doubt would have done some damage.

He pointed at his door, pushed the kid in the direction and growled, "Get into the house. Now!"

Once Talin had disappeared, he pulled the drunk to his feet – the force from his wild swing having landed him on his ass – and shook him like a rag. "Campbell, you're a disgrace to the male race and fatherhood."

"The brat disrespe-ched... me."

"That makes two of us." He pushed the man toward his open back door, "Chrissakes, get out of my sight before I give you what you've got coming. And have a shower, you stink like puke."

***

"Jesus, kid. What set him off like that?"

"He's drunk."

"He's always drunk."

"Yeah, well tonight he was a mean drunk."

"I heard him after you for money. You working?"

Talin went to the fridge and pulled out some

cheese, ham and bread. Next, he grabbed the frying pan from the cupboard and started putting together grilled cheese sandwiches, his favorite snack that surprisingly was always available for him at Murphy's place. "You want a couple?"

"Sure. What kind of job did you find?"

Talin stopped and looked up. Murphy drilled him with his no-nonsense look. "Hey, back off. I'm helping old man Whiteland two doors down clean his yard."

"Okay. Good. Don't look at me that way."

"You don't trust me to keep out of trouble? I'm hurt."

"Bullshit. There's assholes out there who'd like to have a youngster like you on their payroll, selling all kinds of shit. You know what I mean."

"I know. They've already approached me. I told them like you said. That you lived next door and would be on them quicker'n they could call for their mamas if they messed with me. Funny, they haven't come near since."

"Good. Keep your nose clean. Work the jobs you can do helping people around the neighborhood who can't do stuff for themselves. Keep it up and you'll get to college one day."

"Like you, I want to be in criminal justice."

"Not like me. It's a shit job. Most guys at work can't keep a family together and are always broke."

"I was talking the law side, like a lawyer."

"Yeah, well before you start deciding your

future, check with technology to see whether lawyer jobs will still be plentiful down the road."

"People will always break the law."

"True. Criminal attorneys might be around."

Murphy fixed his rye and coke and took the first swill, moaning from the good taste.

Talin watched and grinned. "How come you never get drunk from that stuff?"

"'Cause, I know my body. When to quit before I lose control. And don't say you want to be like me in that way too. It's my one vice, otherwise I'm perfect." A cynical grin broke out over a face not used to smiling."

"Last time I asked, you called it a crutch."

"Guess I'd had my second by then. Listen, squirt, grab a life where you don't need anything but brains and hard work."

"No more with the squirt bullshit. I figure I've outgrown that nickname."

"Fine, Batman, have it your way. Where's my dinner?"

Talin plated the four sandwiches and scored a big glass of milk from the fridge. "I'm staying tonight, okay?"

"Hell, yeah. I wouldn't ask a dog to go back next door the way your old man is tonight. I'll go and mess with him in the morning and see if I can't get him cleaned up."

"You're the only one he listens to anymore."

"That's 'cause I scare the shit outta him."

Murphy took another long swill. "He's an idiot, but not a complete loss. Your mom's death hit him hard."

"Maybe you should tell him what you told me."

"What's that?"

"You growled at me when I was being pathetic. You said, she'd hate to see me become a loser and use the excuse of her dying to behave like a shit. But, if I used her memory to become the son she'd be proud of, she'd be smiling with the angels. Remember?"

"Yeah. It's good advice. Don't know how I got so smart." Murphy chuckled.

Talin pulled a funny face and took a huge bite.

***If you'd like to continue reading this story, go here on the the Universal Link for Amazon: http://mybook.to/SpecialAgentMurphy

Retaliation - Book #1: Her Sweet Revenge Series

Her Sweet Revenge Series
AMAZON
Book #1
by
Mimi Barbour
NYT & USA Today Best-selling author

*** *Warning: This is a series that must be read in order!!*

A virgin librarian with hot-chick potential, the conflicts in her story won't let you put the book down. Be prepared for an all-nighter...

She watches the mob kill her twin and is too frozen with fear to stop them. How can she live with that cowardice eating away at her self-respect? Revenge claws at her sheltered existence until she can't breathe. Though she's naïve, she isn't stupid. When she finds a stash of loot in her brother's gym locker, she has the means.

Now all she needs is the guts to make every one of those low-life gang members pay.

People might think detectives are hard-assed cops with no home life, but Trace McGuire has a dying mom he loves fiercely. Already stressed over his personal problems, he takes a bullet for a virgin beauty hiding while mobsters shoot her brother.

This chick draws out every protective instinct he thought had disintegrated over years on the job and he becomes invested – in her hot body, her plans for retaliation and her fighting spirit.

Helpless, he watches her enter the seedy underworld that'll eat her alive.

Then he sees her fight.

And wonders if they'll survive her.

Praise:

"I am in love with this book and I'll be following the series for more! Mimi Barbour did an awesome job!" ~ *Reviewed by Birna Bjornsdottir*

"Trace – oh Trace how I love you! As soon as he appeared in the story I knew I would fall in love with him and I did! He was a really great character, independent, focused and not afraid to push the limits when needed. Together he and Cass were amazing!

I really cannot wait to read more from this author in the future and highly recommend this story! You will have a hard time putting it down once you have started!" ~ *Reviewed by Katie_83*

"Ms. Barbour has written a gripping story about one woman's quest for justice. She has deftly created marvelous characters that pull you into their story. This is a suspense-filled, full-bore non-

stop action ride that you will absolutely love."
--Reviewed by Colorado Avid Reader

Chapter One – Retaliation

What the hell was she doing following her brother, especially at night? Cassidy Santino didn't do darkness. Not in the slums of a city like Las Vegas when, molasses thick, it threatened and terrified.

Gagging, sweating, she'd reached the end of her backbone. Thoughts of giving up and retreating gobbled up the small amount of bravery still hanging on by a thread, making her hesitate. Then worry for her twin, Raoul, kicked in.

Biting her lip, she eased forward so she could see around the rickety fence into the semi-lit alley behind a big warehouse. A group of men milled about in a circle. Two of them were head-to-head in a heated discussion. Adrenalin kicked in when she saw her brother step out of the circle.

Raoul's shoulders were hunched in the same way he'd hold himself when their father had intimidated him as a boy. She watched him flinch and start to turn away. Then the man he'd been arguing with let out a bellow, backhanded him across the face and shoved hard. Before she could get her bewildered brain to accept the incident, Raoul went down and the other men crowded in and began kicking him.

No! Stop!

Her mind screamed the words, but her voice didn't connect. It froze. When she opened her mouth fear struck her mute. Though she tried to release her rage, to force sound past the blockage in her throat, not even a peep escaped. She'd never felt so useless in all her sad, ineffectual years. Forcing her limbs to move, she fell forward onto her knees but couldn't get her leg muscles to function.

Infuriating seconds ticked by as she watched the men work her brother over like he was a soccer ball, rather than a human being.

God! Please...

Movement, shuffling, a voice called out from another direction. "Police. Stop what you're doing and back away. Get your hands up. Do it now!"

Thank you, Lord! Confidence arrived with the authorities, and Cassi felt a flood of energy. Springing to her feet, she started forward. Before she went two steps, one of the assailants stepped over to Raoul, extended his arm and a gunshot changed the rest of her life. She heard her twin grunt and saw his body jerk.

"No!"

Fear vanished under her instinctive urgency to

get to Raoul. She ran. To help him, save him, give up her life for him. He was all she had in the world, the only one who mattered.

Blinded by grief, unaware of the loud gunplay going on around her, she fell to her knees next to his lifeless form. Before she had a chance to understand the danger, a man dashed out, swept her to the side and covered her with his own body.

"Keep down." Rough, his hands hurting, he pushed her head under his chest while she wiggled to get back to Raoul. "Stop it. You'll get us both killed." His voice, hard and angry drew her attention. She shook away from his hand and looked at him, trying to explain that the injured man was her brother and he needed help. When their eyes met, the bit of light from the building's illumination revealed his face.

Deep blue eyes, encircled with a dark outer ring of pure determination, penetrated for an instant, an order clear and visible that only a man in command could produce. Compelled to obey, but overridden by her need to get to Raoul, she kept pushing at him, until she felt him jerk and heard his grunt of pain.

One of those monsters had shot her rescuer. Disbelief overwhelmed and in seconds the relentless fear returned. Imprisoned and helpless, the horror of the moment clawed at her sanity. Surrendering to its magnetic lure, darkness claimed her, and she knew no more.

***If you'd like to continue reading this story, go here on the the Universal Link for Amazon: http://mybook.to/sweetretaliation1

About the author, Mimi Barbour

MIMI BARBOUR: New York Times & USA Today Best-selling romance author has written nine series and over 45 books. She lives on the beautiful East coast of Vancouver Island and writes her books with tongue-in-cheek and a mad glint in her eye. The fans all agree that it's the fascinating characters she creates which makes her writing so entertaining and brings them back for more of her magic.

"The favorite part of my job is meeting the characters from each new book. Designing them the way I want and having them act however I think they should. It's thrilling, especially when most of my make-believe folks are so very interesting. They're fun and surprising, and in most cases, people I would love to interact with in reality."

Contact me

Amazon author page: http://bit.ly/ MimiBarbourAmazon

My website: http://www.mimibarbour.com/

Or follow me on twitter: https://twitter.com/ MimiBarbour

Or on Facebook: Mimi Barbour Fan page

Please sign up for my fun Newsletter: http://bit.ly/ MimiBNewsletter

or

Write to me anytime. I love to hear from my readers xo
mailto:mimibarbour66@gmail.com

Manufactured by Amazon.ca
Bolton, ON

15448057R00194